BLACK
PRIVILEGE
PUBLISHING

ATRIA

ALL THE

SMOKE

ALL THE STARS, ALL THE STORIES, NO APOLOGIES

MATT BARNES AND STEPHEN JACKSON

BLACK PRIVILEGE
PUBLISHING

ATRIA

NEW YORK   LONDON   TORONTO   SYDNEY   NEW DELHI

BLACK PRIVILEGE PUBLISHING
PUBLISHING
ATRIA

An Imprint of Simon & Schuster, LLC
1230 Avenue of the Americas
New York, NY 10020

Copyright © 2024 by Matthew Barnes and Stephen Jackson

All rights reserved, including the right to reproduce this book or portions thereof
in any form whatsoever. For information, address Atria Books Subsidiary Rights
Department, 1230 Avenue of the Americas, New York, NY 10020.

First Black Privilege Publishing/Atria Books hardcover edition October 2024

BLACK PRIVILEGE PUBLISHING / ATRIA BOOKS and colophon are trademarks
of Simon & Schuster, LLC

Simon & Schuster: Celebrating 100 Years of Publishing in 2024

For information about special discounts for bulk purchases, please contact Simon &
Schuster Special Sales at 1-866-506-1949 or business@simonandschuster.com.

The Simon & Schuster Speakers Bureau can bring authors to your live event. For more
information or to book an event, contact the Simon & Schuster Speakers Bureau at
1-866-248-3049 or visit our website at www.simonspeakers.com.

Interior design by Timothy Shaner, NightandDayDesign.biz

Manufactured in Thailand

1 3 5 7 9 10 8 6 4 2

Library of Congress Cataloging-in-Publication Data has been applied for.

ISBN 978-1-6680-4813-9

ISBN 978-1-6680-4815-3 (ebook)

To our lost family members who aren't here to celebrate with us:

Ann Barnes, Donnie Jackson, Dawndre Buckner, Donald Buckner Jr.

Contents

ALL THE SMOKE

Introduction

IT'S JULY OF 2023, and Matt Barnes and Stephen Jackson just wrapped up an interview with Los Angeles Clippers head coach Tyronn Lue, a conversation—held at Blue Wire Studios in Las Vegas—that marked the 200th recording of their hit series **ALL THE SMOKE**.

You might be a fan from that journey. Or you might have picked this beautiful book up from a shelf or your friend's coffee table and are now wondering: What the fuck is **ALL THE SMOKE**? And Stephen Jackson? The guy who connected on a right hook—a *clean* right hook, to be perfectly clear—to the jaw of a fan during an NBA game? And Matt Barnes? The dude who drove "ninety miles just to whoop a nigga ass"?

 Yep. Those guys. And together, they've created a monster.

ALL THE SMOKE is an award-winning video series hosted by fourteen-year NBA veterans Matt Barnes and Stephen Jackson. In each episode, they're joined by a new pop culture icon, and they uncover who these superheroes really are. See, most of these icons, as well as Barnes and Jackson, were assigned labels by the media throughout their careers. But

these people are so much more than what we think they are. They're parents, sons, brothers, proud Black men, dream chasers, risk-takers, hard workers, lovers, competitive as a motherfucker, grateful, humble and absolutely everything in between.

A lot of public figures are misunderstood. What you hear about them often isn't true. Sometimes it is. But most of the time it's not. So through **ALL THE SMOKE**, Barnes and Jackson have uncovered countless new perspectives, stories, and insights. They've allowed the world to meet a new side of their favorite stars: their true selves.

And it turns out, a whole bunch of people want to know what these people are actually like. Duh! Across two hundred–plus episodes, **ALL THE SMOKE** has racked up billions of views, tens of millions of podcast downloads, millions of social media followers, and a whole lot of that cheddar, baby. They've signed several multimillion-dollar deals with legacy media companies. And now Simon & Schuster, a publishing company founded in 1924, decided the show was good enough to turn it into a coffee-table book. So sit back, roll one up (if you get down like that), and enjoy the ride.

But first, let's turn the tables on the hosts:

So, let's just start with how you guys first met.

MATT: So, Jack gets traded to the Warriors in '07. Obviously, we crossed paths when we played against each other, but never really knew each other. We were struggling as a team, so they made a trade and brought Jack and Al Harrington in.

And as soon as I looked at Jack's lips, I knew he smoked, so I knew we were gonna be okay. It was burnt lips at first sight.

STAK: This dude . . .

MATT: Shit, literally the first day, we started kicking it. Obviously, we made history that season by becoming the first number eight seed to beat a number one seed [the Dallas Mavericks]. But we really bonded on and off the court. We would go watch film at Jack's house, fellowship, smoke, and have drinks. We were inseparable.

I think where we went from teammates to brothers was when my mom died at the beginning of the next season. My mom died at the end of November. And it was just a fucked-up time. And Jack was the one guy that, daily, was checking on me, bringing me food, coming by to smoke, making sure I was okay. My mom and his mom were really close, which made our friendship even stronger. And I think from there we just became brothers.

Before you guys became teammates in 2007, what did you know of each other?

MATT: To be honest, I knew Jack could hoop. I knew he was a hooper. But at that point, everyone kinda knew Jack from the Malice at the Palace brawl. But what I saw was he was down for his teammates, and that's kind of always been my motto. So, knowing that about him, and seeing his lips, I knew it was going to work.

STAK: I didn't know much about him, but I knew we were similar in the way we played the game. **I knew we both didn't give a fuck about much.** We both were great teammates and we both would do anything to win.

MATT: Post-career, we both jump in the media, not really knowing what's next. We were both doing good jobs at ESPN and Fox and getting positive feedback from everyone. Everyone's telling us we got some-thing: "We love your authenticity and your realness." A lot of people were surprised because, again, we did have a certain reputation in the league, but we were able to kind of show the other side. One day I think we were at my house in the Bay, literally just smoking and talking.

And I told him, "Let's do a podcast."

And he's like, "What's a podcast?"

I said, "I don't really know, but I know we can smoke, drink, and kind of be us."

And he said, "Shit. I'm down."

Matt, you've said before that talking to the media during your playing career was kind of like talking to the cops. You felt that your words would often get twisted and turned into a clickbait headline. What exactly was the perception of the media from an NBA player's perspective?

MATT: The media is hit-and-miss. Not everyone is good and not everyone is bad. But when you have a certain reputation at the time, and social media doesn't exist yet, what was written about you became the narrative of who you were as a person. Luckily, towards the end of my career, with social media, we both kind of got to show who we were as people. And then, fast-forward to trying to create a platform, we wanted to be able to tell our own stories. And I think, for so long, people have told our stories, and we just figured it was time to create a safe space where people could come and tell us about themselves. It's not third-person. It's not through someone else's eyes. It's through their true story and mouth. I think we've created a safe environment, which I think is really key. People can come, relax, let their guard down, and truly tell the world how they feel.

STAK: I was scrutinized by the media. I was painted as a person that I'm not my whole life. So I think that's why God opened these doors for me to be able to speak my truths and control my own narrative. Because what they painted me as a player, I was far from. I mean, you can't be a thug and a guy who's a cancer of a teammate. And in the same breath have Tim Duncan call you "the ultimate teammate." That doesn't sound right.

I was judged from one incident for being a loyal teammate. But everybody that played basketball, that grew up playing basketball, you were taught that way. One teammate fights, you all fight. So I just carried it on my whole life. And I'm glad I'm in the media now. It's not about what you do, it's what you do after. And they expected the opposite from me.

What are the earliest memories you guys have of the first few days of ALL THE SMOKE?

STAK: They didn't even want me at first. I wasn't their guy at first.

MATT: Oh, you knew that?

STAK: You told me.

MATT: Yeah. They didn't know a duo was what they were looking for. So I spoke in *The Resurgence*, the DeMarcus Cousins documentary, and got a chance to meet Eric Newman [director], who became our first producer on **ALL THE SMOKE**. He said that his friend, Brian Dailey, was starting a new section of Showtime called Showtime Basketball. He said that I'd be great there. I didn't even know Eric. Weird how shit works.

Maybe a month later, I sat down with Brian at the Loews hotel in Santa Monica and just cold pitched him the idea. I wanted to create a safe space, like a man cave, where you could drink, smoke, and talk about not just sports but life. I feel like some of the best conversations you'll ever have are in situations like that.

I told them that it's me and Stephen Jackson. There weren't a lot of us out there in the space yet, so I think they were a little hesitant about it.

I said, "If it's not me and him, it's nothing." And they weren't expecting that. So after I told them that, they're like, "Okay, we're gonna take a chance."

It started with JR Smith. I think he was our first guest, and that kind of just set the tone. And from there, we have Kobe Bryant, Kevin Durant, Steph Curry—they gave us an opportunity, and we came out the gates really strong.

And then you look at us nearly two hundred episodes later with Magic Johnson, Charles Barkley, Will Smith, Jamie Foxx, Snoop. You name it, we've had them. **I put our guest list against any show, not just podcasts, but any show, period.**

I thank Jack. Where I'm strong, he's weak. Where I'm weak, he's strong. We don't fight for who is who. We just both play our lanes. We both play our roles. I'm the business brain. Jack is the one that keeps the room light. So we both carry the show and carry the weight in different ways and I think that's why we've been so successful. There's no egos. There's no jealousy. We're both us, and it works.

STAK: A lot of guys want to do this, but they're forcing the chemistry. There's a lot of room in this space, but you can't force chemistry. The love is real here. The respect is real here. And we play our roles. We don't overstep. I'm proud to say that I've never been in one meeting for contracts or anything involving **ALL THE SMOKE**. Not one. People laugh at it when I say that, but I think that's a flex. Because how many people can you trust like that? I am my brother's keeper, and my brother is the same. So people can try to do the things we do, but they can't have the authentic vibe and love we have because this shit is just natural.

Last question: What do you hope people take away from each episode of ALL THE SMOKE?

STAK: I just hope people learn something. Each one of our guests, we're also fans of. We want to learn more about them. We want to know something about them that we didn't know before we had them on the show. And we want to hear some stories about experiences in their life that might touch us or could help somebody watching. Everybody's going through different things in life. But each one of our guests has been through something that's a testimony for them and that's motivated them to be great. So that testimony might help anybody watching our show. And I think that's something that we always do. We try to touch a serious point in our guest's life so they can talk about a real experience, because somebody out there is going through that same thing.

MATT: I just hope people appreciate our work. I think we've worked hard to create this lane for not only us but we've inspired a lot of other athletes to do the same. So we just

hope that people just appreciate our grind, appreciate our effort, and appreciate the product that not only us but our team has worked hard to put forward.

You don't normally see coffee-table books with guys like us in them. Again, this is another first, so to be teamed up with such a historic book company like Simon & Schuster is a blessing. We're just kind of giving people a different vibe and different energy when it comes to the coffee-table book. And that's what we've been trying to do with the show. So we try to go above and beyond, be unique, be us, be real. And I hope that people can feel that through this book.

STAK: Coffee-table book boys, cut.

Upbringing

1

we make

There was this reporter one time . . . I had made a lot of big shots when I was with the Spurs. And they were asking me like, "Well, it's your first time in these moments. How have you been dealing well with pressure?" I said, "Well, you know where I'm from. I'm from Port Arthur, Texas. And in Port Arthur, Texas, we make love to pressure." —STEPHEN JACKSON

love to pressure

JASON "WHITE CHOCOLATE" WILLIAMS

JASON WILLIAMS: Where I'm from. It's like the white folks live right here. Then the high school. Then the Black folks. I spent most of my time on the Black side.

MATT BARNES: I could tell.

STEPHEN JACKSON: Duh.

GARY PAYTON

MATT BARNES: You was talking shit to everyone all while still running your team. Where does that shit come from, man?

GARY PAYTON: You know what? It's coming from those streets of Oakland, man. That's why. I grew up like that.

MATT BARNES: The Town.

GARY PAYTON: I grew up in them streets. I used to go to every neighborhood and get down with people, man. My daddy used to be right there talking shit with me, and he used to back me up so niggas couldn't get up and really get down on me. Then my brother was there, too, so people was real, real mad at me because I could get down and I could back it up, and I used to kill them. So it used to be fun to me. You know what I'm saying? I could do it and talk crazy.

So when I brought it to the league, they didn't know what the hell to do with it. So I took it to advantage, and then I still started killing them. It was fun to me. That shit was hella fun just to basically know I could control somebody with my mouthpiece and affect them in the game.

JASON WILLIAMS's flashy handles and swagger earned him the nickname "White Chocolate." He brought a streetball style to the NBA and was universally respected by his peers throughout his twelve-year NBA career. His career includes a championship with the Miami Heat in 2006.

GARY PAYTON is known as one of the best defenders and trash-talkers of all time. Over his seventeen-year NBA career, he earned nine All-Star nods and nine All-Defensive selections. He's one of only a few guards in NBA history to win Defensive Player of the Year, the highest honor a defender can achieve.

3

CARON BUTLER

MATT BARNES: Your childhood . . . born and raised, Racine, Wisconsin. Talk to us about your upbringing and your struggle and just your perseverance to be able to, even though there's a bunch of crazy going on and some happening to you, being able to make your way through it.

CARON BUTLER: Like a lot of young people, just intrigued by all the wrong shit that was going on out there. And I felt like I had to be involved in pretty much everything from hustling and carrying pistols to just trying to mimic the men in my family or who I thought were my mentors, everybody ahead of me. And then from those experiences I was incarcerated. I think it just really humbled me, slowed me down. Obviously it saved my life, but it slowed me down like a motherfucker because I had to really just look at life slower. I was becoming a failure to the people that sacrificed the most for me. My mother, my grandmother. I already had a kid at the age of thirteen, so I was like, Damn, her father's a felon already. And it's like how do you process that shit?

MATT BARNES: Hold on. I didn't mean to cut you off. You had your first child at thirteen?

CARON BUTLER: Yeah, had my first child at thirteen and I just grew up without a father, so I didn't want my habits to continue down that path. So I had to really make a judgment decision where I already knew what the outcome of the path that I was leading was going to lead to. I was going to continue to get incarcerated, somebody was going to blow my back, or I was going to have to do something to somebody. So fast-forward: I just said, I'm going to just try this square straight-and-narrow shit. I'm just going to try this lifestyle and see where it leads me.

Like a lot of young people, [I was] just intrigued by all the wrong shit that was going on out there. And I felt like I had to be involved in pretty much everything from hustling and carrying pistols to just trying to mimic the men in my family or who I thought were my mentors, everybody ahead of me. —CARON BUTLER

DAME DASH

DAME DASH: I'm from 109th and First, which is 1199, but if you ask me what's your block, I would say it's 142nd and Lenox.

STEPHEN JACKSON: Hustling mentality.

DAME DASH: Completely.

STEPHEN JACKSON: Where do you get that from? The environment?

DAME DASH: A hundred percent. In Harlem, it's about getting money and looking good while you getting money.

DAMON DASH is a pioneer in the hip-hop space. An entrepreneur and record executive, Dash cofounded Roc-A-Fella Records alongside Jay-Z.

DRAYMOND GREEN

My junior year, I lost some weight, I got more athletic, and I really started rocking. Ended up being my best year of high school because my senior year my ankle was fucked-up. I was fat as hell. And so I always wanted to go to Michigan State since I was a kid. My aunt went there. She was the number one player in the country. She went there and I used to go up as a little kid. I was scared of Sparty but I always used to tell my momma, "I'm going to go to Michigan State." I was the little badass kid, scared of Sparty, scared of Chuck E. Cheese. I was scared of everything, but I used to always tell them that I'm going to go to Michigan State.

DRAYMOND GREEN is a four-time NBA champion and the engine of one of the greatest dynasties in NBA history. He's regarded as one of the best defenders and fiercest competitors in NBA history.

AL HARRINGTON

AL: To be honest. I ain't start playing basketball till I was a freshman in high school. Growing up I didn't really have hoop dreams. It wasn't . . . like I wanted to play in the NFL. You know, my goal was to play for Notre Dame and play for the New York Giants. But, when I got to high school, I was 6'4". And when I got to this new school, everybody just thought I could hoop. So they put me on the team as a freshman. So, on the freshman team, my nickname was "Big Daddy."

MATT: I heard a couple of people still call you that.

AL: That's not true.

AL HARRINGTON spent sixteen years in the NBA and is also the founder of Viola Brands, a booming cannabis company named in honor of his late grandmother. Harrington was a key member of the 2007 "We Believe" Warriors squad alongside Matt and Stak.

LaRUSSELL

MATT: Talk about your upbringing in Vallejo. You know, I'm born and raised in San Jose but then moved to Sacramento. So I came past this. I was close to this. About a highway but I got family out this way. But it is different out here. I try to tell people Vallejo—

LaRUSSELL: It's different.

MATT: The Bay, they're all different in their own ways, but they're just way different than everywhere else.

LaRUSSELL: Yeah, I mean, I think it's just the energy. I feel like the energy of Vallejo feels like Mac Dre and E-40. Like when you hear they music and the way they talk—

MATT BARNES: Valley Joe.

LaRUSSELL: and the way they dress, the slang, like you get a very good representation at a Bay. Like it's a . . . I don't know, it feels like a party.

LaRUSSELL THOMAS saw a corrupt music space and took matters into his own hands. At just thirty years old, he's been a pioneer to bring power back to artists from major streaming companies. He's also the founder of Good Compenny, a Bay Area–based nonprofit independently funded and operated by creatives.

DEJOUNTE MURRAY

When you are just a product of your environment, you just go with the flow. You trying to make it to the next day. Survival. And that had to be my mindset at ten years old, eleven years old, right away. Even before that. But I always had good people like uncles, my grandma, and all the aunties and stuff that looked after me. We just was bad kids running around the neighborhood, running around the house. But as it got to ten, eleven years old is when I started getting active. Always was around older people. And the first time in juvenile was eleven, and then thirteen, fourteen, fifteen, and I think the last time was fifteen. They knew I was always talented in basketball and the judges always just had something for me. It was already written from God or something. Like I was always getting smacks on the wrist. And I'm watching my homies get thirty years, forty years, fifty, all the way to eighty years. Partners I talk to till this day every day. And I remem-

DEJOUNTE MURRAY is a seven-year NBA pro and currently plays for the Atlanta Hawks. He spent much of his childhood in Seattle in and out of juvenile prison. After finally leaving that life behind, he's now one of the brightest young players in the game.

ber the last time I went. This is a story I never told anybody. I'm in juvenile, and they detain me. They keep me in for an extra thirty days. I'm thinking I'm getting out. Mind you, I'm supposed to be at practice, I'm supposed to be at school. So there's a big game coming up. It's Rainier Beach versus Bothell. Zach LaVine went to Bothell. So the whole city, they knew I was younger and he was older, getting ready to go to UCLA, but they knew the talent was there, so they was hyping the game up. I'm in juvenile. I miss the game. Biggest game of the year, biggest game in the city. And for me, it wasn't because they was hyping the game up; it just was opportunity to go out, showcase myself, and show that I'm ready to be the next guy, knowing that Zach's head in the college and obviously the NBA. So I'm in there and I'm just thinking like, Well, this ain't the life I want. This is not the life I want. Even if it ain't basketball, I got to figure it out. And obviously I had a great support system. My uncles, they built a plan for me. They, like, we about to move him out the hood. We about to move him with my auntie, rest in peace. She was 107 years old. I lived with her. And they was like, We going to move him out the way. We going to homeschool him. And the rest was history, bro. I got out, moved away, moved away from my family, the hood, everything. It was like I was ghost. I was gone. Gym, house, gym, house, every day for three years, sophomore to senior year. And I just seen them tables turn, and when you start doing the right thing, I feel like God bless you. And God started blessing me each and every day.

KOBE BRYANT

We had a really competitive household with my cousins and my father and my uncle and stuff. We were very competitive, and you had to really, really work to just survive. That's with swimming, that's playing basketball, that's playing video games, whatever. I mean, it was a shit-talking family. When you lose, you not only lose, but you get embarrassed while you lose, you know what I mean? So I grew up in that kind of environment. So you had to work hard just to kind of keep your head above water sort of thing.

> When you lose, you not only lose, but you get embarrassed while you lose, you know what I mean? —**KOBE BRYANT**

SNOOP DOGG

STEPHEN: Your mom was big in music, too, right?

SNOOP DOGG: Oh, man, please believe it. Mom sang in the church, led the choir, did all that good stuff. My whole family was connected to music, but nobody actually made that breakthrough to actually get a big deal and become a big star. They was a lot of writers, a lot of behind the scenes, a lot of artists that was connected to my family, but I was the first one to actually break the mold. But it's the years of them not making it, which was the spirit of me pushing through.

STEPHEN: Right, they paid the dues.

SNOOP DOGG: Come on, man, you know you can't do it without the forefathers and the grandmothers and the people that did it before you to get you the foundation.

VINCE CARTER

My junior year is when I found out T-Mac was my cousin. So he comes out and he goes to the draft and he's coming in to work out. And I don't even know if you all know this stuff, he's coming in to play pickup because he was at Mount Zion, which is right there in Durham and he's looking to play pickup. We're playing pickup at Carolina all week.

I said, "Hey bro, you can use my locker, whatever, store your stuff." All week, because I knew him from back in the crib.

On Thursday he said, "Bro, I'm not going to be here on Friday because I'm going for a family reunion."

"All right, cool. Whatever, I will see you next week when you get back," just like that, I wasn't going because I was in school, you know what I'm saying? I was back in school playing pickup.

MATT BARNES

STEPHEN JACKSON

VINCE CARTER

Bro, he sits at the table with my grandmother, they get to talking, she's like, "Oh, so you went to school in North Carolina?" She was, like. "Oh, my grandson plays college ball."

And he's like, "Oh, for real? Who's your grandson?"

She's like, "Vince Carter."

Bro, I get a call from Granny. "What's up, cuz? What's up, cuz?"

"Wait a minute, who the hell is this?"

"This Mac, man, this T-Mac. What's up, cuz?"

That's how we found out we were cousins.

PENNY HARDAWAY

I got blessed because the city of Memphis, on every street corner, every park, it was like no fouls. You had to hoop. If you weren't proving yourself, you couldn't get on the court, and a lot of times with the older cats, you have to pass the ball a lot and play defense and get that ball to the people that was really doing it until you got your chance. So you have to build that reputation with the guys before they even allow you to start shooting. And that made me tougher. That made me mentally tougher, physically tougher, because there were no fouls and you had to defend. I'm so thankful that I grew up in that type of era.

ANFERNEE "PENNY" HARDAWAY played fourteen years in the NBA and earned four All-Star selections. Born and raised in Memphis, Tennessee, Penny first burst onto the scene in his hometown at Memphis State University (now the University of Memphis). Currently, he is the head coach at his alma mater.

SHAQUILLE O'NEAL

MATT BARNES: Take us back to your upbringing, your family dynamic, military kid, so moving around—

SHAQ: Born and raised in Newark, New Jersey. High-level juvenile delinquent. Got out of there just in time. This was around the time where people stopped using their hands.

MATT BARNES: Picking up guns.

SHAQ: They'd be a chain and knife and then a pistol started coming out.

STEPHEN JACKSON: Your big ass definitely would have wanted that.

SHAQ: Yeah, exactly.

STEPHEN JACKSON: Everybody fighting you.

SHAQ: By the grace of God, moved to Germany. Got away from that. Right? Two, three years in Germany. Now the only thing I could focus on is basketball. I'm terrible. 6'9", cut from the freshman team, cut from the sophomore team. Again my father comes in the house: "Get your ass up. We're going to go see this college coach. See if you can get a scholarship." It was Dale Brown. So I went in there and I said, "Hey, Coach, I need help. I ain't made the team." Blah, blah.

MATT BARNES: What age are you at this point?

SHAQ: This is, like, thirteen. 6'9", I can't play. I got bad knees. I got Osgood-Schlatter.

MATT BARNES: Osgood-Schlatter.

SHAQ: I got the brown knee brace with the hole in the middle.

MATT BARNES: The old-school joints.

SHAQ: I'm slow as hell. I can't do anything. People are laughing at me. So Coach Brown writes me. I do everything he says. The next year I still didn't make the team. So I sent him a letter: "Man, I'm going to just join the Army. They're right. I can't walk and chew gum at the same time, I can't do it." Now we leave and I come back to Texas. I go to a small high school in Texas. Our team is terrible. I make the team. Aw, shit. I'm starting to get a little confident. Then my dad had take me to see Jon Koncak and now everything just changed overnight for me. Everything just changed overnight for me.

Being that I was a hip-hop kid, I had a little rhythm. I'm not doing what Kareem . . . I'm not doing those sky hooks. I like this Magic cat. I started working on my little handles. Right? Then when I first started dunking . . . I never wanted to dunk. Junior year I got 45 at three. I'm killing the little dudes that I'm playing against. I finger roll it and I miss. So my father walks on the court, he calls a time-out. I'm cool then, Public Enemy out, I got the Flavor Flav, like I'm cool. I'm cool.

He takes me outside. He said, "Yo, man, what the fuck you doing?"

I said, "Man, I'm just, you know, you know I'm working on my little ma—" Whap! Smacks me. Ain't no Magic. Be Shaquille O'Neal. That's when I started dunking right. The reason why I've always dunked so fierce, because I was mad at him. Middle of the floor, talking about.

MATT BARNES: Because of that.

SHAQ: And I wanted to tear the rim down, but it was just regular dunks. Then I go home and he making me watch the college games. I'm watching Syracuse play. Sherman Douglas throws it to Rony Seikaly. He dunking, but he getting his legs up. I was like, "Oh, okay." So the next game my father is there. I'm dunking and getting my legs up. So what I learned from that, people started doing that.

STEPHEN JACKSON: Hell yeah.

SHAQ: I said, "Oh, okay. I got something there." So that's when I just started dunking, dunking, dunking, dunking, dunking, dunking, dunking, dominate, dominate, dominate.

RZA

STEPHEN JACKSON: Brownsville, New York, in the '70s, '80s, what was that like?

RZA: Come on, man, Brownsville, listen, Mike Tyson comes from Brownsville.

STEPHEN JACKSON: Mike Tyson, I was just going to say that.

RZA: Hold on, Riddick Bowe, Mark Breland. Fighters, you know what I'm saying?

STEPHEN JACKSON: Yeah.

MATT BARNES: Fighters for real.

RZA: Listen, you've got to fight. That was, on a reality, the toughest streets I ever walked in my life.

ROBERT FITZGERALD DIGGS, a.k.a. **RZA**, is a rapper, actor, music producer, and filmmaker. Many consider RZA the brains behind Wu-Tang Clan, one of the most prolific and successful musical groups in rap history.

JAYSON TATUM

JAYSON: I love St. Louis. St. Louis is one of the biggest reasons why I am who I am today. And I always go home as much as possible and show love whenever I can. Just because it got me to where I am. We've all got stories and situations of a lot of guys that came from the same place as us, but a couple mistakes away that they didn't make it. And I tell people all the time, people ask me, like, "Why are you so confident?" or "What was your biggest fear growing up?" I always wanted to play basketball and be in the NBA. And I never felt like I wasn't good enough or I didn't have the talent. I tell people my biggest fear, all the time, was just growing up in St. Louis just being at the wrong place and the wrong time. That was like a real fear for me.

STEPHEN JACKSON: I tell people that all the time, bro.

JAYSON TATUM: Yeah, it's real. Being in the wrong place at the wrong time is scary, especially back in St. Louis. I thank God every day I was able to live out my dream.

WILL SMITH

STEPHEN JACKSON: I got a short story. When I was younger, we drove from Texas and rented a RV. I'd never been outside of Texas.

MATT BARNES: You?

STEPHEN JACKSON: Me and my family, my grandfather.

WILL SMITH: You?

MATT BARNES: News flash.

WILL SMITH: You was in a RV?

STEPHEN JACKSON: And we drove from Texas to San Diego. But this why I remember the trip. So that drive, you get super-bored. So we stopped and we were kids. So soon as

we stopped, I'm ready to run and do something. So I punch my cousin and take off running. He chases me: "Ha ha, you ain't going to catch me." I ran dead into a tree. So for the next day and a half, I ain't got no skin on this side. I'm looking like Two-Face on *Batman*, I got skin on this side. I'm just sitting there like: I'm ready to go home.

When I get in my car, I don't listen to no rap. I put on Marvin Gaye to the Pointer Sisters. I'm in there rolling to what my moms cleaned up on Saturday with. . . . That was the type of music that wrote the soundtrack to my childhood. —THE GAME

THE GAME

STEPHEN JACKSON: What other music did you grow up on?

THE GAME: I'm really a oldies R&B dude. When I get in my car, I don't listen to no rap. I put on Marvin Gaye to the Pointer Sisters. I'm in there rolling to what my moms cleaned up on Saturday with. When you wake up on Saturday and you hear that, you know what I'm saying? You had Anita Baker and Mary Jane Girls and the vacuum. That was the type of music that wrote the soundtrack to my childhood.

Compton rapper **JAYCEON TERRELL TAYLOR**, a.k.a. **THE GAME**, carried West Coast hip-hop in the 2000s through his raw narratives and lyrical prowess. His discography is highlighted by *The Documentary* (2005) and *The Doctor's Advocate* (2006).

T.I.

STEPHEN JACKSON: Let's talk about your childhood on the west side of Atlanta.

T.I.: Man, just a little badass, nappy-haired, light-skinned boy. You know what I'm saying? I ain't really . . . I mean man, I was very small and always just inquisitive, always getting into shit unnecessarily. But I was very smart in school with academics and stuff. And a lot of people always ask, "How can you be so smart and then get in so much trouble at the same time?"

And I think that that was . . . the two became tethered together, probably in kindergarten and third grade, when I'm kind of small compared to other people in the class and shit. Light skin, come to school fresh every day. And when the teacher called on me to read, I read fluently. So it was a lot of hate from that. So I had two choices. I could either pretend to be not as smart, so you know . . .

STEPHEN JACKSON: Ruff it down.

T.I.: Yeah, dumb it down. Or I could show you motherfuckers that I'm just as smart and get in just as much trouble as y'all. And I chose the latter. Both of my intellect and my troublesome nature kind of grew at the same rate of speed.

GERVONTA DAVIS

MATT: You mentioned it a little bit, losing people along the way. Rough childhood in Baltimore. Take us back to your childhood and what the scene was like and what actually inspired you to get into boxing?

GERVONTA: Coming up normal just an inner-city kid. Mother and father was on drugs and things like that. And my mother left us in the house by ourselves, and protective services came, grabbed us, and they split us up. And once my grandma fought to get us back. I was always the aggressive one because I was younger. So I was much more aggressive than my oldest brother. I was always fighting a lot. I used to fight for my brother because we was the new kids on the block, and we was brought up under our grandma. We didn't have our mother and father. So it was

GERVONTA "TANK" DAVIS is one of the most prolific boxers in the world. He has held multiple world championships in three different weight classes and has some of the most ferocious power and knockout ability in the sport.

stuff like we had Reeboks and the other kids had Jordans and Nikes and things like that. So I always used to fight. I used to fight in school. So one time I was fighting in front of my house, and my uncle saw me fighting. So he took me to the boxing gym.

MATT: Not to cut you off, how old were you at that age?

GERVONTA: I want to say seven.

MATT: Oh, damn. Early.

GERVONTA: I was seven. Yeah.

STEPHEN JACKSON: It must have been a flawless victory.

MATT: Yeah, right?

GERVONTA: Yeah. So we was fighting and things like that. So he took me to the gym. And when I was going to the gym, it wasn't really about the fighting or boxing at that time. It was really about me getting that love at the gym that I wasn't getting at home because my grandma, she was moving around too much and things like that. So she didn't have time for us. So I just got that love. I got that father figure. I had other kids in the gym, like brothers and things like that. So I was always fighting in the gym too. So I just grew up and just, they started being family.

AMAR'E STOUDEMIRE

MATT BARNES: Your upbringing. Florida boy. Bounced around a lot from school to school. Talk to us and tell us what your childhood was like.

AMAR'E STOUDEMIRE: Man, it was a struggle, bruh. My childhood was a major struggle, man. My mom was always . . . she was always getting locked up. So she was in and out of jail basically all my childhood life. My dad died when I was twelve. My brother was a gangster. He was always in the streets. He got locked up for selling drugs. And so I had to basically raise my little brother on my own at times. And so I went to . . . When I played basketball, I didn't play organized basketball until I was fourteen. But I played at the parks all the time.

AMAR'E STOUDEMIRE played fourteen years in the NBA and earned six All-Star selections and five All-NBA nods. He's one of the best big-man dunkers of all time, and was a leading force in the Phoenix Suns' "7 Seconds or Less" era in the mid-2000s.

MATT BARNES: What did you hold on to, or what inspired you, or helped you get through? I mean, as a fourteen-year-old starting to play basketball, you're becoming a man. But there's so much up and down and, like you said, inconsistency in your life. What was the thing that kept you on track? Because at the end of the day, I think you only really got a chance to play, what, two years of high school basketball?

AMAR'E STOUDEMIRE: Yeah, I first played organized basketball at fourteen, and I was drafted at eighteen. So it was a quick turnaround between my first game—

MATT BARNES: But you didn't really get to play that whole four years, though, right? I mean, you missed some seasons in high school, right?

AMAR'E STOUDEMIRE: Yeah. Yeah, exactly right. I only played two years of high school basketball.

MATT BARNES: Yeah, so to think about, you were the number nine pick in the draft after playing basketball for just two years. That shit is fucking crazy.

PHIL HANDY

MATT BARNES: Most influential basketball figure in your life?

PHIL HANDY: My brother. Unheard-of. C. L. Handy Jr. He was my closest brother and taught me how to play. He really took me under his wing when I was a little kid and he would just beat the shit out of me, man. My number one goal was to beat him one-on-one and I don't think I ever did. That drove me, but he inspired me to really take the game of basketball and try to do something with it.

PHIL HANDY is an underground legend in basketball as one of the best player development coaches in the game. He went to six consecutive NBA Finals from 2015–2020, winning three (2016, 2019, 2020).

Mothers 2

you can do

JAYLEN BROWN

JAYLEN BROWN: You can curse on this show?

MATT BARNES: You can do whatever you want.

STEPHEN JACKSON: Yeah, hell yeah. Fuck yeah.

JAYLEN BROWN: Yeah, my mom, she's the realest nigga I know.

STEPH CURRY

MATT BARNES: I heard a rumor that your mom fined you $100 for every three turnovers, is that true?

STEPH CURRY: Yeah, three turnovers and I had to give her $100. So she got a lot of handbags, let's put it that way. I be throwing those crazies. She'd be yelling at me, but she'd be mad happy at the same time.

STEPHEN CURRY is the greatest shooter to ever grace this earth, and over his fifteen-year NBA career he's won four championships, two MVP awards, and has ten All-Star appearances.

STEPHEN JACKSON

What people don't know is, sometimes in Black neighborhoods, telling my mom is worse than taking me to jail. I just want to let y'all know that.

MATT BARNES

I fought so much, my mama had to come be the yard duty at my school.

BRADLEY BEAL

Mom put the ball in my hand and she taught me how to shoot. To this day, she blows my phone up if I have a bad shooting night. "You need to get your ass in the gym. You ain't doing what you're supposed to do."

JAYSON TATUM

My mom, she a supermom. My mama . . . she a gangster for real [. . .] I love my mama to death. My mom a gangster.

BRADLEY BEAL is a twelve-year NBA pro currently playing with the Phoenix Suns. He's made three All-Star games and is one of several elite players from St. Louis, Missouri.

SHAQ

I'm sort of like you guys, I'm a mama's boy.

SHAQUILLE O'NEAL, a.k.a. **SHAQ DIESEL**, a.k.a. **SUPERMAN**, a.k.a. **THE BIG ARISTOTLE**, is one of the biggest—literally and figuratively—icons basketball has ever seen. Over his nineteen-year NBA career, O'Neal won four championships, three Finals MVPs, and one regular season MVP. He is one of the most dominant forces in sports history. He's also a gifted marketer, television personality, entertainer, and entrepreneur.

> My mama . . . she a gangster for real.
>
> —JAYSON TATUM

And she told me, "You made your bed, you got to lay in it. —DRAYMOND GREEN

KENYON MARTIN

Just being in Dallas, man, growing up in the projects, it's all we knew. We never owned a car growing up. Had to catch the bus to go to grocery stores and do a lot of things. No dad there. Me and my older sister. But Mom tried. She did what she had to do. Things were rough for a lot of reasons. We grew up in an area where people dabbled in certain things and it derailed the whole situation, man. Yeah, so we fell victim to that. But, nah, I stuck by her no matter what. No matter what was going on, that was my lady. People ask me the best time I had in the NBA, I say, "Draft day." They, like, "Why?" Like, "Be able to take care of Lydia. Be able to give her things she ain't ever had, man."

KENYON MARTIN played fifteen years in the NBA and is regarded as one of the fiercest competitors of his generation. Born in Saginaw, Michigan, Martin was heavily influenced by the "Bad Boys" Detroit Pistons. If you watched him play, the Bad Boys influence was clear.

DRAYMOND GREEN

My freshman year, I was trying to transfer because I wasn't getting the clock I wanted and I fucking knew I should have been playing. Every time I played, I played well. But I had Delvon Roe in front of me who was the top five recruit at my position and the same class with me. And then I had some seniors ahead of me, but I earned my minutes. But we played at Ohio State once that year. And I ain't played, that was the only game I didn't play at all, but I didn't play at all. I called my mom crying on the bus like, "You got to get me the fuck out of here." And she told me, "You made your bed, you got to lay in it." And so I just kind of locked back in. I ended up playing great through the tournament and then, shit, the rest of my career I just got better and better. And the rest is history.

RAJON RONDO

STEPHEN JACKSON: What is your heritage? Where does the name Rajon Rondo come from?

RAJON RONDO: My mama just made the shit up. It's a unique name that I appreciate to this day. It ain't nothing. My uncle's name is Rodrick, and I think she started with . . . she knew where the R was from. It's just made up.

MATT BARNES: This nigga said, "That shit was made up."

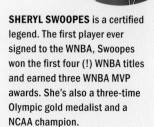

RAJON RONDO is the epitome of a true point guard. Over his sixteen-year NBA career, Rondo racked up over 7,584 assists, ranking him fourteenth all time. His résumé is stacked: two NBA championships, four All-Star games, three assist titles, and four All-Defensive selections.

SHERYL SWOOPES

Sports were huge in my life. Like I said, I grew up with two older brothers. And the only way my mom would really let me leave the house is if I told her I was going to go play basketball with my brothers. My mom was very, very, very strict. And at the time, I was just. like, "Damn, she's just so mean." That's what I thought. But looking back on it, I'm so glad that she raised me the way she did, because at any moment I could have taken the wrong turn and ended up being somewhere different, just like a lot of my friends were. And I think people talk about this a lot. But I think more so for girls or women, sports was a huge part as far as helping me with my self-confidence and my self-esteem. I grew up in a very small town. We didn't have a lot. And people told me all the time that I couldn't do something, one because of the color of my skin. That I wouldn't be good enough because I was a girl, because I was too this, I was too that, I wasn't good enough. But because I believed in me, and I had the right people around me, meaning my mom and my brothers, it didn't really matter what everybody else said to me because I was determined that I was going to be successful and prove all those people wrong. And it still happens today.

SHERYL SWOOPES is a certified legend. The first player ever signed to the WNBA, Swoopes won the first four (!) WNBA titles and earned three WNBA MVP awards. She's also a three-time Olympic gold medalist and a NCAA champion.

KEVIN GARNET

My mom is a straight-up G. My mom was the first part of me learning what hard work and pushing through and being mentally strong, she was my first and probably my only decent example, in which I obviously took from players and stuff, but when it came, I never got to see MJ practice or prepare, but I prepare with laser focus and laser concentration, so that when I got on the court, I knew exactly how it was going to be and I was following that vision.

My mom is a straight-up G. —KEVIN GARNETT

STEPHEN JACKSON

A lot of people don't understand what you learn from your mother. Not having a father there, people don't understand how hard it is for a mother to play that role. To keep us out of trouble when we want to rebel and be men at a young age. It's really hard. So when we do make it, that's really our only goal. To change our mom's life. People don't know the dues and the stuff she went through for us to even be here to even have a chance to make it to the NBA. So, I totally feel you, because me and Matt had the same relationships with our mom, you know what I'm saying? Matt's dad was around, but my dad wasn't around. I know, even though you got this money, it don't stop, because you have more things that you want to do, and that money just makes you hungrier.

DeMARCUS COUSINS

Without my mom, there's no telling where I'd be, honestly. I don't know how she did it. Mother of six, so all the same house. Her work skills was insane. Thug it out during the day with us, and night shift she working doubles.

Without my mom, there's no telling where I'd be, honestly. —DeMARCUS COUSINS

RICKY WILLIAMS

Really, my mom was more like a dad anyway and so I just had like a mom, that was just about it. And she just taught me how to be tough. And above everything, she just taught me that life ain't going to be fair, don't expect it to be. Make the most of every situation.

RICKY WILLIAMS is one of the greatest running backs in football history and a pioneer in cannabis awareness. Williams's career was cut short because of the NFL's harsh stance on cannabis. Since his retirement, he's launched his own cannabis company, Highsman.

KEVIN HART

MATT BARNES: Who were some of the people that inspired you growing up? Like shows or comedians?

KEVIN HART: I know the answer is always, you want to go to the biggest comedians, but the biggest inspiration is my mom before you can even get to comedy. Because you got to understand drive when you're talking about entertainment. Any level of entertainment, any level of accomplishment in life, there's a high level of drive that you need to have in you to attach, to set goals,

to try to accomplish whatever. Are you willing to stay true to it, work on it, and go through the ups and downs to get to whatever the end is? So my mom, the reason why I say she was the inspiration is because without the constant repetitive conversation of start what you finish, or finish what you start, or we don't quit . . . What we don't do is leave stories untold. I got a bunch of these things in my head for my mom. You don't leave room for people to complete the sentences that you left incomplete. Finish your sentences, finish the things that you put your mind to. That's always stuck with me.

KEVIN GARNETT

KEVIN GARNETT: And we thank God, Shaq was raised right, because, oh, my God.

MATT BARNES: Right. That's a big motherfucker.

KEVIN GARNETT: You all haven't played against a pissed-off Shaq. What?! Thank you. Thank you, Mama O'Neal, we thank you. Thank God for that, seriously.

ISIAH THOMAS

There's a street named after my mom in Chicago. My mom was . . . she was a gangster. She was the real deal.

SNOOP DOGG

Shout out to all of the great mothers that raised great men that don't get credit. Because a lot of these great men had great women in their lives that shaped and molded them and gave us some concrete to stand on.

ISIAH THOMAS is one of the most iconic basketball players of all time. Standing at just over six feet, Thomas is a two-time NBA champion, twelve-time All-Star, and the face of the "Bad Boys" Pistons. Outside of hoops, Thomas has an extensive business portfolio, highlighted by Isiah Real Estate, Cheurlin Champagne, and One World Products.

Shout out to all of the great mothers that raised great men that don't get credit. —SNOOP DOGG

CHRIS WEBBER

CHRIS: I didn't know we were going to get traded from Sac to Philly. That was the worst season. I think I drank more than I ever drank and wanted to leave the league. It was depressing. But what was crazy about all that is that the best times we had there was after the games. We'd go meet up after with your mom.

MATT: And my mom came in there and we got drunk.

CHRIS: Me and his mom, good times, man. And it was right before you found out that she was sick. We had some real talks, like while you were in the other room. And she's telling me about your childhood and telling me how she loves you and telling me that you're funny and hardheaded. And I was asking that: "Did he get in trouble when he was little?" She'd be like, "Yeah, he's mischievous."

She told me about one party. You were charged and motherfuckers were in the backyard and selling weed or something at the same time. And she was like, "I realized how much he made." And I was like, "Did you ever think he would make it to the league?" She was like, "I thought he'd play football. He was always a hard worker." But me and her had some wonderful times, man. And that's why you are real, 'cause of your parents.

MATT: I miss her.

JOHN WALL

JOHN WALL: You don't think like those little talks or one-on-ones would mean so much. But the feelings like "I'm tired. I'm at peace . . ." It's like, why would I want her to suffer and keep fighting? I'm not the one that got to be in that body so, you kind of accept it but you're still like, God, my best friend, my mom, gone. So for me, like, I had my dad for nine years in my life but most of the time he was in jail. And then had my mom for twenty-nine, so, it was like, I know what it feels like not to be on both ends and not have either one, so, like, my main goal is seeing the aspect of how quick things can be taken away, so that's why I

JOHN WALL is one of the most electrifying point guards in NBA history. Prior to his pro days, Wall was a high school phenom and spent one year at the University of Kentucky. Over his eleven years in the NBA, Wall earned five All-Star nods and led the Wizards to several playoff appearances, a rarity for the franchise.

try to cherish as much moments as I can with my son . . . I got a "Dear Mama" tattoo on my back. It's crazy, because I got like a "Mama's Boy" on my chest, one of my first tattoos I got because everybody's always calling me a mama's boy. Then when she was going through the cancer and I'm just seeing her fight. I'm like, Mama is just so dope to me, I'm like my mom's going to always have my back and always be watching over me. So that's what I put on the back of my neck. The only thing that really irks me until this day—and you know you probably feel the same, Matt—is like, Did I do enough? Like, Did I make my mom happy? That's the only thing that be like, Yo, did I have enough fun with my mom? Did I do enough? And I have a dope assistant that's always be like, Yo, don't ever question yourself or think about that because just go back and watch the pictures and seeing your mom smile and see that.

MATT BARNES: Yeah, man.

JOHN WALL: So that kind of clears my mind a little bit. I put a picture of me and my mom at the White House Correspondents' Dinner and, like, she got to meet Michelle and Barack. So, like, to take my mom to that, that lets me know I did something special.

MATT BARNES: I love that. I was telling the crew before we got on the air today, I went back and watched Game 6. The "We Believe" season when we beat Dallas in the clinching game and this motherfucker Jack is on fire and I think I hit him with an assist [and] he hit his sixth three-pointer. Dallas called a time-out and somehow the camera . . . Like I said, I had never seen the game. I was watching the TNT feed, the camera panned right to my mom in the crowd, and she was up, jumping around, screaming, hands above her head, and I'm like, that shit gave me instant chills, like, what are the chances out of 20,000 people in the arena, Jack was the motherfucker to hit the shot. I didn't even hit the shot, it just happened to pin on my mom and dad. I'm like, Damn, that shit is crazy.

That's how Jack and I became brothers, man. Like, he was there every single day. Talking and doing whatever you need and you need that. At first, I was closed off to the world. I tried to play a day after. I was closed off, quiet, but then when I started to open up and talk and I really felt like I kind of started to heal a little bit and share the good memories and the fun times and that's what Jack was there for me. We would just chop it up and it really helped me have a different outlook. Although, it still hurt, it just gave me a different perspective on shit.

JOHN WALL: Yeah, it's definitely going to always hurt, but, like you said, being able to talk about it and having somebody you can talk to . . . And you can tell the kind of bond y'all have. You know, I mean even just by this show. But, I've seen y'all way before this. How y'all bond. You can tell that bond ain't fake.

DJ QUIK

JACK: Talk about how important your mom is to you. And early in your career, you told a story about how she kept you home the night of the Tyson fight.

DJ QUIK: Yeah, the big bad Death Row guys came to my house to get me to go to the fight and I didn't want to go. I just felt something, it was like instinct. I went to the studio. So they at my house knocking on the door, tell Moms, "Hey, we know he in there. Tell him Suge want him to come to the fight. Tell him to bring his bitch ass outside." They just talk so disrespectful. My mom said, "If you all don't unhinge that door, I'm going to have the police in here in five minutes." She was not having it and I was not even there.

She was mom with the finger. And sure enough, that was the night that Tupac got killed. Them old Creole women, they know too much. Their instinct, they just . . .

JACK: Feel it.

DJ QUIK: Yeah. It's a gut feeling for them. And she always told me: Follow your first mind.

SNOOP DOGG

My mother raised me to love people. I was born in the '70s, so I was raised in the era where it wasn't about color. I had friends that was white, Hispanic, Asian, everything. You get what I'm saying? I was taught to love people.

DAWN STALEY

There's nothing more gratifying than making your mother proud.

DAWN STALEY is one of the most accomplished players and coaches in women's sports history. During her playing days she was a two-time NCAA Player of the Year and three-time Olympic gold medalist. As a coach, she's won two NCAA championships and another gold medal. Staley is currently the head coach at the University of South Carolina.

Inspiration

3

a brother that

was a player of all players

DEION SANDERS

DEION SANDERS: I didn't have a favorite team, but I had a favorite player. Dr. J was my guy. He was a doctor. He was called a doctor, and he didn't have a PhD. You talk about a brother that was smooth. A brother that was suave. A brother that was a player of all players.

STEPHEN JACKSON: Still to this day.

DEION SANDERS: To this day. Doc was so cool back in the day, man, that he took the imagination of a young cat from Fort Myers, Florida, man, and I just love everything about Doc. How he carried himself on the court and off the court and how people perceived him, what they saw when they saw him. I loved it. He was my guy. He was my guy growing up.

Nobody epitomizes swagger quite like **DEION SANDERS**, a.k.a. **PRIME TIME**. Sanders was a Pro Football Hall of Fame cornerback and a Major League Baseball outfielder. He's the only person in history to play in both a Super Bowl and World Series. Currently, he's the head football coach at the University of Colorado, Boulder.

JAYLEN BROWN

MATT BARNES: I saw you working out with T-Mac. Is he someone that you modeled your game after? Who did you look up to coming into the NBA?

JAYLEN BROWN: T-Mac.

MATT BARNES: That was it.

JAYLEN BROWN: T-Mac was it.

MATT BARNES: Think about that . . . Tatum's is Kobe. His is T-Mac. You put them together . . .

STEPHEN JACKSON: Ooh, ooh.

KEVIN GARNETT

STEPHEN JACKSON: Your early years, who did you pattern your game after?

KEVIN GARNETT: Oh, man—

KEVIN GARNETT is a twenty-one-year NBA veteran, 2004 MVP, 2008 champion, and founder/host of *KG Certified*. Garnett embodies toughness, passion, grit, and being the ultimate teammate.

STEPHEN JACKSON: Coming in the game.

KEVIN GARNETT: Coming into the game?

STEPHEN JACKSON: Because a lot of people will say, "There was no KG before KG." So who did you pattern your game after?

KEVIN GARNETT: I look at Webb and Big Dog, even though we're in the kind of same generation, but those are my older brothers. I was thinking like, Man, what if Magic came from the hood? What if Magic had a DMX kind of attitude with this shit? One thing I loved about Webb, Webb used to dunk it on you—

STEPHEN JACKSON: Oh, yeah.

MATT BARNES: Yeah, yeah, yeah.

KEVIN GARNETT: It ain't no laying it up, he's going to put you in the basket. I wanted to be like Webb. Webb was like this big-ass like Charles Barkley, but he was a chocolate nigga.

RASHEED WALLACE

Well, growing up, of course, there's only one doc in Philly, Dr. J. That was my man. Because, one, everybody in my house loved him, my mom, my brothers, all of that. Everybody loved him.

PAUL PIERCE

MATT BARNES: So, growing up in LA, obviously you're a Lakers fan, right?

PAUL PIERCE: That was a must. I wore a Lakers sweater, I'll show you all pictures. I've got a Lakers sweater I used to wear every day to school. It was a hoodie that I got. I mean, who could not be a Laker fan? I grew up right down the street from the Forum, right there in Inglewood, watching Magic. I hated the Celtics. It was just, like, you're from LA, let alone Inglewood, where the Forum is, of course you're a Laker fan.

STEPHEN JACKSON: How can you not be?

PAUL PIERCE: How can you not be? So that's what made it real ironic when I got drafted to the Celtics, and I didn't even work out for the Celtics. So then when I look back at my career, man, it's like, damn, some shit is meant to be.

PAUL PIERCE, a.k.a. **THE TRUTH**, was one of the most clutch players in NBA history. He played nineteen years in the league, was named to ten All-Star games, and won a Finals MVP in 2008. Pierce nearly lost his life in September 2000 when he was stabbed eleven times in a nightclub. He returned to the court a month later and played all eighty-two games in the 2000–01 season.

That was a must. I wore a Lakers sweater, I'll show you all pictures. I've got a Lakers sweater I used to wear every day to school. It was a hoodie that I got. I mean, who could not be a Laker fan? —PAUL PIERCE

STEVE NASH

My hero growing up was Isiah Thomas from as far as who I wanted to emulate. He had everything, but he wasn't jumping over people. So I was like, Okay, there's somebody that I can try to emulate. He was quick. He used his skill level, his creativity, his competitive nature. Like the fight in him was incredible.

STEVE NASH is one of the greatest floor generals to ever step on a basketball court. A two-time league MVP, Nash was the engine of the infamous "Seven Seconds or Less" Phoenix Suns team that helped revolutionize basketball. Nash played eighteen years in the league, made eight All-Star games, and was inducted into the Basketball Hall of Fame in 2018.

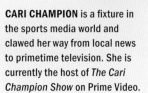

CARI CHAMPION

I love Oprah. When I was a kid, I saw Oprah. I was like, I want to do what this lady is doing because she looks like my auntie.

CARI CHAMPION is a fixture in the sports media world and clawed her way from local news to primetime television. She is currently the host of *The Cari Champion Show* on Prime Video.

My hero growing up was Isiah Thomas . . . the fight in him was incredible. —STEVE NASH

JA MORANT

Man, it's a lot of guys, actually. I probably studied every top guard that played the game. Some to just throw out there, I watched a lot of Nash, I watched a lot of Kidd, I studied Penny, AI for that killer mentality. Growing up AAU days, I was watching Kobe and 'Bron, then watching Rondo with that Celtics team, how he was facilitating the offense and getting guys open looks. That's what kind of made me fall in love with passing the ball just to be able to affect the game in so many ways. I feel like it makes you more dangerous.

JA MORANT emerged from mid-major Murray State University and immediately electrified the NBA. Five years into his career, he's made two All-Star games and was named Rookie of the Year in 2020.

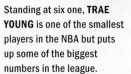

TRAE YOUNG

Yeah. Yeah. I mean, obviously Steph is one, but Steve Nash was the main guy. Steve Nash is one of my favorite players. He's someone who I watched a lot of film of.

Standing at six one, **TRAE YOUNG** is one of the smallest players in the NBA but puts up some of the biggest numbers in the league.

WIZ KHALIFA

MATT BARNES: Who were some of your inspirations?

WIZ: I feel like my whole existence is just a combination of everything that I've seen and loved. I love groups, so Bone Thugs-N-Harmony is one of my favorite groups, Wu-Tang, Dipset, like just the whole . . . having your own slang and your own logo and your own way of dressing, that always influenced me. Busta Rhymes is one of my huge influences. I loved his videos and how animated he is and just being yourself. The

energy, the performance onstage, is crazy. Jay-Z, swag on stage. You know what I mean? So these are all little things that I pick and choose from that I love. Cam is my favorite artist out of everybody, just as far as swag, attitude, lyricism. People try to say that he don't really *rap* rap . . .

STEPHEN JACKSON: Please.

WIZ KHALIFA: He dumbs it down, like, you know what I mean? Like Cam's that nigga.

STEPHEN JACKSON: He rapped, though.

WIZ KHALIFA: Yeah. Cam is hard.

CAMERON JIBRIL THOMAZ, a.k.a. **WIZ KHALIFA,** is an American rapper, singer, songwriter, and actor. Khalifa has been a mainstay in the hip-hop world since his emergence in the late 2000s.

ISIAH THOMAS

STEPHEN JACKSON: Let's stay on the west side. Let's talk about Lord Henry. How big was he in your life and how nice was he?

ISIAH THOMAS: Man, so my older brother, Lord Henry, I think he may still hold the Catholic school scoring record. Went to St. Philips. Back then, the NBA wasn't on TV like the NBA's on TV now. So you only admired the people in your neighborhood or your older brothers.

STEPHEN JACKSON: The locals.

ISIAH THOMAS: Yeah, the locals. And every now and then you may hear about Dr. J, and in your imagination, you think, This is a Dr. J move, but you ain't never really seen him. But my brother Lord Henry was so smooth, man.

STEPHEN JACKSON: The name alone, you had to be cold with a name like Lord Henry.

MATT BARNES: Lord.

ISIAH THOMAS: Yeah, yeah, yeah. My mom and my dad, they had high hopes for us. He got turned out, though. He got turned out on heroin. Ended up dying several years ago. But, man, you're talking about a pretty jump shot, between-the-leg dribbles, behind the back. And the way I was taught to play the game and the way he taught me to play the game, it was all spiritual.

And I can remember him and my second-oldest brother, well, third-oldest brother, Larry, it's like, "Junior, you know, you just can't play the game. You got to feel it."

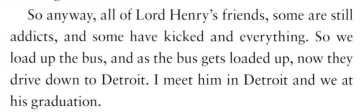

Junior, you can't just play the game. You got to feel it.
—ISIAH THOMAS

And I remember when Lord kicked and he said, "I'm going to go back to school." He went back, graduated from college, and I'll never forget. You've been on the west side, right? The night before graduation, I rented a bus and the bus was meeting on Fifth Avenue in Jackson. And he was graduating from school in Detroit. I think it was Phoenix University? You know that—

MATT BARNES: Mm-hmm, University of Phoenix.

ISIAH THOMAS: Online. Yeah, that online thing. So I rented a bus and I had the bus show up on Fifth Avenue in Jackson at 4:00 in the morning, 3:00 in the morning. I want everybody to be there at 3:00 in the morning, bus going to leave at 4:00, going down to Detroit so we can watch Lord Henry graduate at Ford Field.

And I'll never forget, bus driver called me up, like, "Hey, man, you sure I got the right address? You sure I'm in the right location?"

I'm like, "Yeah, man, you in the right location."

So anyway, all of Lord Henry's friends, some are still addicts, and some have kicked and everything. So we load up the bus, and as the bus gets loaded up, now they drive down to Detroit. I meet him in Detroit and we at his graduation.

And I'll never forget, man. My brother walking across the stage, had his cap and gown on. He didn't know we was going to be there.

And all his friends started hollering, "Lord Henry! Lord Henry!" And, man, he broke down on the stage and just started crying. Crying like a little baby, man. That was one of the most beautiful days that I remember. So when you talk about Lord Henry, yeah, it's basketball playing, but the fact that that dude went back to school . . . and then he just died a couple years ago, his organs just shut down all up. The heroin and stuff, it just, body just collapsed. But—

MATT BARNES: Rest in peace. Condolences, man.

STEPHEN JACKSON: Yeah, man.

ISIAH THOMAS: Yeah. Thanks for bringing him up.

STEPHEN JACKSON: For sure, man.

TYREEK HILL

MATT BARNES: Being on the smaller side, but playing bigger, anyone you idolized growing up? Was it smaller guys or was it just people who could play?

TYREEK HILL is one of the most explosive players in NFL history. He's made eight Pro Bowl appearances in eight years and won a Super Bowl with the Kansas City Chiefs in 2020.

TYREEK HILL: I admire anybody who could play football, dog. But for me, the person that really stands out to me was just Steve Smith. He was a very undersized receiver just like I am. He went to JUCO kind of like I did, same path, same mindset. I feel like he was just a dog. If you watch his NFL films or just anything, like, he was in a fight down there. Every snap with cornerbacks or coaches or whatever the case may be, he wasn't backing down for nobody. So, yeah, definitely Steve Smith.

JAYSON TATUM

Kobe was my Jordan. He was my favorite player. He was the reason I started playing basketball.

LAMAR ODOM

You said who I wanted to be like? Magic Johnson.

Ambition 4

You're not going to sleep and then wake up years later and be successful . . . You've got to work. You've got to work. **—KOBE BRYANT**

to work

KOBE BRYANT

You're not going to sleep and then wake up years later and be successful . . . You've got to work. You've got to work.

DeMARCUS COUSINS

This is a nonstop grind. People just see the fame, the glamor, the money, the cars. They don't see that grind behind the scene. It's a lot of talented ballplayers out here, but it ain't many lasting ten, fifteen years in the league. It may not be because of talent; it may not be because they not fast enough. They can't handle the grind. It's a commitment.

DeMARCUS "BOOGIE" COUSINS played eleven years in the NBA and was one of the most skilled big men of his generation. Boogie made four All-Star games and earned two All-NBA selections. He's currently the co-host of *Bully Ball* and the founder of *Boogie's Comedy Slam*.

They don't see that grind behind the scene.
—DeMARCUS COUSINS

STEPH CURRY

MATT BARNES: Getting a chance to play with you guys in the '17 season and always competing against you. When I see you guys in practice and how hard you shoot, and the workouts you go through, and you guys really don't miss. I tell people, when they say, like, "That shot was lucky Steph took." I was like, "No, Steph's practiced that shot every single day after practice." You mentioned something earlier. People only see the finished, three-point, mid-range process, but some of the workouts you and KD were doing, and then Klay was on his court doing his thing. Like, it was some of the most unbelievable shit I've ever seen.

STEPH CURRY: When you're around greatness like that, it just continues to motivate you and encourage you because you don't want to be the dude that's not continually getting better. And so we all push each other whether we talked about it or not. It's just like a presence thing. When KD walks on the court, when I walk on the court, Klay walks on the court, Draymond with his mindset and his passion, it's just contagious, and everybody just wants to one-up the ante a little bit.

I tell people, when they say, like, "that shot was lucky Steph took." I was like "No, Steph's practiced that shot every single day after practice." —MATT BARNES

You know why I get up at 4:30? Because
I live in LA and there's a cat in New York
getting up at 7:00. —KEVIN GARNETT

KEVIN GARNETT

You know why I get up at 4:30? Because I live in LA and there's a cat in New York getting up at 7:00. He up already, working already. Actually, if he got up at 6:00, I'm an hour and thirty behind this cat. So I used to think like this. Amar'e in New York, there's some cats on the East Coast, and they're already working in Atlanta. Damn, I'm late. So I used to hit the beach at, like, 4:30, and then I used to go through all this with the workout and the gym, and then I'm done by, like, 12:00, right? And then I used to think, like, Damn, yo, they don't even respect that a nigga get up and do this every day like this. So I started losing appreciation for them appreciating me. I was like, You know what? Somewhere somebody else is going to show you some love. Or so you hope so.

RACHEL NICHOLS

One of the things I tell people who want to get started in my field . . . a lot of it is just to fucking work harder than anybody else. You have to be the last person in the room. If you do that, it's not a guarantee that you're going to do great. But you're probably not going to do great without it.

> One of the things I tell people who want to get started in my field . . . a lot of it is just to fucking work harder than anybody else. —RACHEL NICHOLS

RACHEL NICHOLS is an award-winning journalist and sportscaster. She's covered the NBA and NFL for nearly thirty years. In 2014 she was named "the country's most impactful and prominent female sports journalist" by *Sports Illustrated*.

DRAYMOND GREEN

Being a second-round pick, for me, I felt like I should have been a first-round pick. I won National Player of the Year. Like Anthony Davis . . . all those guys was in college the year that I won National Player of the Year, and I went second round. National Players of the Year don't go second round. I went second round and there's all these questions. Ironically, they asked who I was going to guard. Which ain't do shit but motivated me. What position was I going to play? That motivated me to do what I've done and try to make positions meaningless. But it was always fuel to my fire. But I said it before. I still to this day can name all guys drafted before me because that shit will never stop driving me. But I said being a first-round pick just didn't fit my story.

STEVE NASH

I mean, it comes down to wanting and having a passion to do it. Like, I had an absolute passion and competitive nature to want to compete, wanting to be out there, wanting to play as long as I could. And so when you have that passion, you're willing to make sacrifices. And so I was willing to make sacrifices, willing to learn. I'm looking into all sorts of different ways that I could recover or perform or whatever it may be. So, yeah, it started with a passion, and then a curiosity, and then I just continued to dial it in, and fortunately was able to play through my thirties.

WALLO

I'm just a grinder. If you grind out anywhere on the earth, you're going to fucking win. Now, if you going to bullshit, you want to be lazy, you want to be "cool," you want to be "lit." You ain't got shit coming. So my whole thing is like, I don't care where I'm going to go. I'm going to just grind and everything is going to pay off.

At age seventeen, **WALLACE PEEPLES**, a.k.a. **WALLO**, was sentenced to twenty years in prison. After his release, he joined forces with his cousin Gillie Da Kid and launched the popular series *Million Dollaz Worth of Game*. Wallo has grown an audience of millions on social media.

> Now, if you going to bullshit, you want to be lazy, you want to be "cool," you want to be "lit." You ain't got shit coming. —WALLO

JULIAN EDELMAN

That was my career. I had to grind and grind and battle through injury. And then once I got some more opportunity and earned more opportunity, that's when things went well.

JULIAN EDELMAN was a fixture of the New England Patriots dynasty in the 2010s. A twelve-year pro, Edelman won three Super Bowls and amassed over 6,500 receiving yards.

KENDRICK PERKINS

My mama died when I was five. She was shot and killed by her best friend. My daddy bounced and went overseas, so I was raised by my grandfather and my grandmother. My grandfather was making $300 a month. My grandmother was making $40 a week being a maid. My grandfather cleaned up the church. My motivation was that I got to get them out of this situation. So the first thing I did when I got my check, I bought them a motherfucking crib before I bought myself a house.

KENDRICK PERKINS played fourteen years in the NBA and won a championship with the Boston Celtics in 2008. After his retirement in 2019, he transitioned to the media world and is currently a prominent television host on ESPN.

DJ QUIK

To go from making two hundred fucking dollars, bro, a week, to fucking $10,000 a night onstage . . . I got addicted to making more records. I wanted that to never stop because I knew back then this shit is not going to last forever. So let me hit, strike while the iron is hot. Keep going.

DAVID BLAKE, a.k.a. **DJ QUIK**, is one of the greatest rappers/producers of all time. His role in the boom of West Coast hip-hop is seldom discussed, but Quik played an integral role in the movement. Quik's sound is unique and features a slick flow and funky rhythms.

GILLIE AND WALLO

GILLIE: See, that's one thing I can give Wallo, though. Wallo, all of us, might have been seventeen, eighteen, Wallo might have been fifteen, but you wouldn't have thought Wallo was fifteen. You feel what I'm saying? He was always tall. Then this nigga got a tattoo on his neck. "Fuck bitches, take money."

WALLO: That's when I was young.

GILLIE: Niggas didn't even get tattoos.

WALLO: This was ninety—

MATT BARNES: That's what the tattoo really said?

WALLO: Yeah. Right here. It's faded, you can see. "FBTM." That's when I was young and crazy, I was crazy. You understand? I was, like, fifteen?

STEPHEN JACKSON: "Fuck bitches, take money."

GILLIE: Yeah.

WALLO: That was my mindset at the time.

GILLIE: That's what we was on, bro.

STEPHEN JACKSON: "That's what we was on?"

GILLIE: That is what we was on.

WALLO: I just wanted some pussy and some money. That's all.

GILLIE DA KID is a rapper and songwriter based in Philadelphia. He was one of the members of a seven-person rap crew known as Major Figgas. Today, he co-hosts the popular series *Million Dollaz Worth of Game* with his cousin Wallo.

PAUL PIERCE

MATT BARNES: September 24th, 2000, stabbed eight times, nearly died.

PAUL PIERCE: It was so bad that I couldn't even sleep. I would wake up in the middle of the night, this is a story a lot of people don't know. I had to have a twenty-four-hour police surveillance at my house, that's how paranoid I was. All I did was go to the gym and home for, like, a two-year stretch, man. It changes you, dude. You don't know where to go, you don't who to look at. You're on your toes, you're really on your toes. Like, man . . . I'll kill somebody. You know what I'm saying? I was just like that. So I had to channel all that energy towards basketball. I was to the point of losing it. All I wanted to do was go to the gym, so now I'm hours in the gym, because, you know, that's our sanctuary. That time we're in the gym, we don't think about anything else. That very short period we got right there, everything else go out the window. Whether it's girl problems, family problems, money problems, whatever. You know how it is. Y'all know what I'm saying, just that one moment you got out of that day. I turn that into hours in the gym, though, like, four, five, hours in the gym. I didn't want to stop. I didn't want to go home because now that's all I'm thinking about.

SHANNON SHARPE

SHANNON SHARPE: Guys saw how hard I worked, but for me when I played those fourteen years, nothing else mattered. Football was the most important thing. Other than breathing. Football was most important. Not family, not kids. Not brother. Not mom. Not sister. And I make no apologies for what I was able to accomplish in my fourteen years.

MATT BARNES: Who that sound like?

STEPHEN JACKSON: Kobe.

SHANNON SHARPE: Nah. And look, during my Hall of Fame speech, I told my kids, because the kids would come for a couple of weeks during the summer and I promised I'd take them to the amusement park and Six Flags. And I had every intention of doing that.

SHANNON SHARPE is one of the greatest tight ends in NFL history. Today, he's a powerhouse in media with ESPN and The Volume.

But after running for two hours on the track, after lifting for another two hours, I was exhausted. And I know at the time they didn't understand. All they know is that Daddy had just told me another lie. He said he was going to take us and I didn't. But as they got older, hopefully they understood this is how you go to college. This is why you got the car that Daddy . . .

MATT BARNES: Sacrifices.

GILBERT ARENAS

If you want something great, you got to let something go. You got to sacrifice something that's important to you.

GILBERT ARENAS played eleven years in the NBA and made three All-Star games. Although injuries hampered his career, Arenas's peak is up there with any all-time great point guard.

DAME DASH

MATT BARNES: Unfortunately your mom passed from an asthma attack when you were fifteen. Mentally, what did that do to a fifteen-year-old man trying to figure it out?

DAME DASH: Makes you a beast.

STEPHEN JACKSON: Animal.

DAME DASH: Makes you a savage because now you have no fear. When the number one thing you're scared of happens and you could deal with it, you're no longer scared of anything. It just made me fearless because it was like, shit, if I get killed I'd be with my moms.

STEPHEN A. SMITH

STEPHEN A. SMITH: I remember when a cat came, they came to me and they wanted me to have a job in Seattle. I was going to go, unless the *New York Daily News* came. They had a job for me in Fresno. I was going to go unless the *New York Daily News* came. It was like no matter what, whatever the sacrifices that are that need to be made, I think to this very day I've never been married because of that. Because I was always ready to get up and go. Because when you growing up and you poor and you living off tuna fish and Kool-Aid from the time you're in college. You taste government cheese and bread when you younger. You sat up there and watched your mother work two jobs, seven days a week, sixteen hours a day, for twenty years with one week's vacation nonstop. You go through all of that, it's not that love don't matter, it's not that family don't matter. It's none of that, it's that I'm not going back to that.

STEPHEN JACKSON: You become numb to a lot of stuff.

STEPHEN A. Smith: And whatever sacrifices need to be made, I'm going to make to get ahead. And that's always been my approach. So when I talk to professional athletes, particularly those of us that are professional athletes, Black folks, I'm sitting there like, I know your story. I've been through it.

STEPHEN A. SMITH is one of the most prolific journalists in sports history. Born to immigrant parents in the Bronx, New York, Smith grinded his way to the top of the sports media world.

STEVE KERR

To be honest, I'm not sure I ever felt 100 percent comfortable that I belonged. Maybe that's what drove me. I always just felt like I could get cut at any time, and so, as a result, I put in the work and I competed. I just kept sticking around. I ended up playing fifteen years, which is shocking. I still can't believe that my career lasted that long.

STEVE KERR has won nine NBA championships over his thirty-plus-year NBA career. As a player, he won five championships beside the likes of Michael Jordan and Tim Duncan. As a coach, he helped lead the Golden State Warriors to four championships.

RENEE MONTGOMERY

I had to dream it. So when people are "Oh, this has never been done" . . . I'm used to dreaming about stuff that's never been done.

I'm used to dreaming about stuff that's never been done. —RENEE MONTGOMERY

T.I.

STEPHEN JACKSON: At what point did you feel like you caught a break and really got your first opportunity?

T.I.: Man, shit. That wasn't until nineteen, twenty. I was eighteen, nineteen, something like that. You working at something, working at something, working at something, going from this group of producers, these managers, to traveling to New York and shopping your demo with this label, this label, this opportunity. People saying, "Yeah, man, I think I can get us in. I think I can." And then just rejection, after rejection, after rejection, I kind of got discouraged. And that's kind of when I

CLIFFORD JOSEPH HARRIS JR., a.k.a. **T.I.,** is a rapper, producer, and actor born and raised in Atlanta, Georgia. He's a pioneer of "trap music," a rap genre started by Harris and others in the early 2000s that is still running strong today. T.I. is a three-time Grammy Award winner and was a leading figure in hip-hop during the 2000s.

just jumped headfirst into the streets. Probably around fourteen, well, thirteen, fourteen, fifteen. Kind of like, Man, this rap shit ain't going to work. Man, we try something else. You know what I mean? And then I started becoming introduced to people like Master P, you know what I mean? Started researching like rap. Started seeing how people who didn't get signed by majors, how they manifested they own destiny and became the architect. And so that's what we did, man. Me and a group of homeboys, we just hustled and hustled and hustled and used the money every week that we hustled on Sunday to go to the studio and shit, we kind of worked that move until we made it.

LaRUSSELL

STEPHEN JACKSON: 2021 you have 4,000 followers. Now you at half a million.

LaRUSSELL: Sheesh.

STEPHEN JACKSON: But all off the organic hustle. How'd that feel?

LaRUSSELL: Yeah, all off the grind, man. It feels good. You know, I'm somebody who firmly believes in . . . nothing is impossible as long as you work for it. If you do the work, you're going to get the results.

STEPHEN JACKSON: Right.

LaRUSSELL: And we did a shit ton of work. So it's beautiful to see that it actually works.

And it's not just theory.

STEPHEN JACKSON: Not a thing.

LaRUSSELL: A lot of people think people are lucky or people are chosen, but it's like, Nah, nigga. We really did that work.

CARI CHAMPION

I flew myself out to ESPN. Every job I get, I hustle. Ain't nobody been like, "You know what, brown girl, let me fool with you. You so heavy, you so bad. Let me . . ." No one does that now, but everything I've ever gotten literally has been on my own. And I flew myself out to ESPN, I was just knocking on doors. That's what I always tell people. Just hustle. Nothing comes to you. I can't stand people that do nothing. I flew myself out there. I stayed in the little broken-down Bristol hotel. I'd have no money. I had whatever I had, and I just paid for myself to go there and back. And I was there for two days, just sitting in the lobby, waiting for people to beat me. I had no planned meetings. I was like, Okay, whoever wants to come see me, I'll wait. I'll wait. And then that was that. And I got the job. Then my entire life changed.

KEVIN HART

MATT BARNES: Obviously, today, being one of the biggest comedians in the world, one of the biggest movie stars in the world, your grind, your struggle, obviously was tough. Talk to us about your first gig. Because I know that didn't start off too well.

KEVIN HART: Shit, first stand-up gig?

MATT BARNES: Mm-hmm.

KEVIN HART: First stand-up gig. First bad one, first bad one is a famous story, Sweet Cheeks. It was a male strip club. I didn't even know at the time.

MATT BARNES: It was called Sweet Cheeks?

KEVIN HART: It's called Sweet Cheeks.

STEPHEN JACKSON: Hold on, hold on, hold on.

KEVIN HART: Got to take what you can get.

STEPHEN JACKSON: Hold on, hold on. You didn't know it was a male strip—

KEVIN HART: I didn't know it was, it was in Atlantic City.

STEPHEN JACKSON: It was called Sweet Cheeks.

KEVIN HART: It's called Sweet Cheeks.

STEPHEN JACKSON: Okay.

KEVIN HART: Very well, could have been a place that serves apples.

STEPHEN JACKSON: Fuck no.

KEVIN HART: Sour Patch Kids, I don't know. It could have been anything. Could have been the candy house. Well, I don't know. They said they wanted to have a comedy show. I was one of the comedians. I'm out. I'm going.

STEPHEN JACKSON: At Sweet Cheeks.

KEVIN HART: Listen, man—

MATT BARNES: Would you have to wear—

KEVIN HART: I performed at a bowling alley and they was throwing strikes while I was doing punch lines. I can give you bad stories. I did a crab shack . . . I performed at a crab shack and I could hear niggas cracking crabs while I was—

MATT BARNES: Giving a joke?

KEVIN HART: Yes, man. Sweet Cheeks was definitely the worst. Sweet Cheeks, it was this raunchy—it might have been some of the worst, just vulgar people, man. And they didn't want comedy. These people didn't want comedy, it was just a mixture of people that came to drink and the comedy and the comedy show was the shit that they would give the comedians. That was the comedy. It wasn't the comedians, the comedy was them fucking with the comedians. And it was what comedians are bold enough to go. So I was never a bitch about it. I'm going to go.

SHANNON SHARPE

In 1987, I was a sophomore and I remember because we had community phones. I didn't have a phone in my room. And I remember walking down the hall, it was all quiet. I said, "You know what? I'm going to call my grandmother. Nobody's here." So I get on the phone, call collect. Operator comes on the phone. "Yes," I say, "I like to place a collect call to Mary Porter from Shannon Sharpe." Operator comes on, "This is a collect call to Mary Porter from Shannon Sharpe. Will you accept?" My grandmother said no. She said, "I can't pay this $50 phone bill I got right now," and hung the phone up. I remember walking down the hall and tears started to well up in my eyes. My roommate's in the room so I can't let him see me cry and I'm just laying there. I go lay on the bed and I'm looking up at the ceiling and I'm just staring. My friends going out on Saturday, Friday night. I'm going to take care of Granny. So I know what that did to her to tell me, "No I can't accept this call because I got a $50 phone bill I can't pay right now." So I'm laying and I'm thinking. The only thing that I'm thinking, I'm leaving, I'm going to NFL. That was the only thing that mattered. And when I got to the league, the only thing that mattered was football.

PENNY HARDAWAY

MATT BARNES: You're off to New York in '04. What's your thought process as far as knowing you and what you're capable of bringing and what you felt like you can go to the Knicks and accomplish.

PENNY HARDAWAY: I think that was probably the most disappointing time to be in the city, on the biggest stage in the Big Apple, and not be me. I'm out here like a shell of myself, on the biggest stage. And I'm like, Man, why? I just wish that I could just get to a point where I could be me and I just push through it. But I knew I wasn't me, man. And I love New York, and I felt like the fans deserved me at the highest levels. Because you know how New York is, and playing for the Knicks was a huge honor. I didn't take that lightly, but I would also go home and, like, go, Oh, man, I just hate that I'm not me, I'm not myself.

MATT BARNES: Goddamn. What did you do to combat that, you know what I mean? You can keep trying, you can keep pushing, but mentally what did you . . . Because that's what I like to have other people understand. There's so much fucking mental that comes along with this process. What did you do to fight your way out of that or deal with that or handle that situation during that time?

PENNY HARDAWAY: You know what, I said to myself, You're here, let's make the best of it, work your ass off. Give it all you got, don't leave nothing in the tank and then you can go to sleep at night. That's what I did, man.

PAUL PIERCE

Yeah so, I came here with a chip on my shoulder. I wasn't going to wait for nobody, I was just like, I'm here, I'm pissed that these other teams didn't draft me. I'm coming out, this is it. You only get one shot and this was my shot. I need to make a name for myself right now, that was just the fire in me, the competitiveness, and I wasn't going to take a back seat to nobody, that was my mentality, of just, like, either love me or hate me, straight up, this is who I am, this is how I'm going to play every night.

JAMIE FOXX

MATT BARNES: Only the second male in history to receive two Oscar nominations off of two different movies, [and the] first Black, or African American to do it. The only other person to get two was Al Pacino. Talk to us about, we know it was a grind, but in that moment, being that part of history, what did that mean to you?

JAMIE FOXX: Well, in order to get to that history, we had to go back of what I, what I went through, you know. It's sort of like I reference

JAMIE FOXX is one of the greatest entertainers of his generation. He's an Academy Award-winning actor, Grammy Award-winning singer, and is regarded as an elite impersonator.

everything, like, you know, being a rookie on *In Living Color* or with the Wayanses, you know. I was, like, the eighth funniest person. Imagine walking in and you are the eighth funniest person. It was Keenen, it was Damon, it was the fucking Tommy Davidson. Them motherfuckers were incredible. So I had to learn how to really compete.

TAYLOR ROOKS

STEPHEN JACKSON: What has been your evolution and journey in this particular journalism space been like?

TAYLOR ROOKS: Good. Definitely ups and downs. I think sometimes with this, it is a bit of an uphill battle, not just being a woman, but being a Black woman. Always constantly feeling like you have to prove yourself a bit more, to show that you're more than just this girl. Everybody wants to comment about how they look or how they dress or whatever. There's so much substance that goes into being a journalist, and y'all know you cannot fake this, right?

STEPHEN JACKSON: People hate what they can't be.

TAYLOR ROOKS: 100 percent and I will say that forever.

TAYLOR ROOKS is a sports journalist and broadcaster. She currently appears on *Thursday Night Football*, Bleacher Report, and Turner Sports.

CARI CHAMPION

I got my first job in West Virginia. So I drove my little Nissan Altima to West Virginia to be a reporter and I was a one-man band. You see how they got their cameras and tripod? That's what I was doing. Running around West Virginia, filming stories. It was hella racists. People would call me the colored lady. But I loved what I was doing. I didn't care. You didn't care that she was making $2 an hour and you look crazy on TV. I was telling stories and I was living my best life. And I was like, Look, this is what I've always wanted to do.

Kobe

5

this is going to be

Kobe changed the game, man. Kobe changed
Los Angeles, the NBA. —**MAGIC JOHNSON**

one for the books

KOBE BRYANT

MATT BARNES: All right, man. So, shit. Normally we shoot in Santa Monica or in New York, but today we made a special road trip to go see the one and only.

STEPHEN JACKSON: The one and only.

MATT BARNES: Yo, I mean, we had to drive hour and a half in traffic to see Kob'.

STEPHEN JACKSON: It don't matter if we had to drive backwards . . . I'm excited, though. This is going to be one for the books. **ALL THE** motherfucking **SMOKE**.

MATT BARNES: Let's have a great show.

LAMAR ODOM

LAMAR ODOM: He said he was better than Mike.

STEPHEN JACKSON: Huh? He said it? I know he did. He thought it, he thought it. You could tell, though, he felt that way.

LAMAR ODOM: Word, [he said it.] On the back of the bus one day. I said, "What?" Well, you got to understand his drive, it ain't too many dudes that played in the NBA or that's playing ball right now that's [would say that and] really mean it. That in their heart, even that's growing up right now, [that would say] like, "I am going to be better than LeBron James." And that's what he chased his whole life was to be just as good or mentioned with Michael Jordan.

SHAQ

I knew that he had it. And I remember him at eighteen years old telling me he going to be the Will Smith of the NBA. Like, slow down young fellow. But he had a dream. He had a vision.

KOBE BRYANT was an eighteen-time NBA All-Star, five-time NBA champion, and one of the greatest athletes this world has ever seen. Bryant played an instrumental part in the lives of both Matt and Stak, first connecting with Stak at the 1996 McDonald's All-American Boys Game, and with Matt on the campus of UCLA during Bryant's early years with the Lakers.

JR RIDER

When he got in the game he was real . . . he was real . . . I'm just going to say it, "wild," right? He was kind of wild, but . . . I remember calling my brothers at home, like, "Man, I just played against the rawest young eighteen-year-old that's probably out there. I mean, I ain't never played against a young boy that got it like this."

DeMAR DeROZAN

For me, Kob' was my imagination that was a player. Obviously, as I got older and able to look at Michael Jordan, he became one of my favorite players, but growing up when I started to understand and comprehend basketball at a young age, it was from Kob'. Being a Laker fan, we didn't have cable. All we had was channel KCAL 9 when the Lakers played on Channel 9. That was the only fucking channel we had, so I watched every Laker game growing up and Kob' was the one that I gravitated to. For me, to see the start, the fails, I remember begging my dad could we go get a newspaper just so I could see what he said after the game, comments after the game. Little shit like that gave me an emotional connection to one of my favorite players that made me want to push harder when it came to wanting to play sports, especially basketball, seeing how he got better, the things he went through. The culture of LA, for me being thirty-one now, is based around Bean, the energy always being Kobe. Obviously, I always heard the stories like my dad and my uncles always talking about the Showtime Lakers. That's their generation, but for people my age you can't think about the Lakers without thinking about Kobe. You can't think about that.

BRADLEY BEAL

BRADLEY BEAL: So it's my first game playing against him. He's on the wing. I think, I want to say Sasha had the ball. All of a sudden he says, "Sss. Sss."

STEPHEN JACKSON: That's that mamba noise. That's that mamba snake noise.

MATT BARNES: It don't matter how loud the arena is, you're going to hear that motherfucking hiss, and the ball better be in his hands in the next three to five seconds.

LOU WILLIAMS

MATT BARNES: Yeah, so I got a chance like you to play with AI, play with Chris Paul, super-competitive dudes, but to me there's no one more competitive than Kobe.

LOU WILLIAMS: Yeah, that he would say some shit and then the whole was like, like, we had a . . . fuck, he goin' to be mad at me for this, but look, we had a blowout, we got blew out in Portland, and he came in the locker room and he was like, "From now on out, every time down the court, I touch the ball. Y'all gonna learn what it's like to play with Kobe Bean Fucking Bryant." And I'm sitting there looking like, Oh, this mother-fucker's serious.

PENNY HARDAWAY

MATT BARNES: Reflect a little bit on Kobe as a competitor. Did you get a chance to know him well on or off the court? What was your experience like with him and against him?

PENNY HARDAWAY: It's funny, I have a weird Kobe story and I have to say, two of them really quickly. I met Kobe when Kobe was in high school and I didn't know who he was. Obviously, I'm the man in the NBA. I got the Lil' Penny commercial, I'm a signature shoe, I'm on top of the world on [crosstalk] NBA, and he came to me after a Sixers game and asked me what he should do on going to the draft, and, man, I had never known who Kobe was and I felt so bad afterwards because he asked me should he go.

He was like, "Well, should I go?" And I said, "I don't know, young fella. You might need to go to college." This is Kobe Bryant! And he was like, "Well, they're telling me I'm going to be lottery." I said, "Well, if they're telling you you're going to be lottery, dog, then you should go." I changed that, because I didn't know who he was. And a couple of years later, he's in the league, he never forgot that conversation. Magic Johnson has an All-Star game in the summer, everybody knew those Magic Johnson games were crazy.

MATT BARNES: Midsummer Night's.

PENNY HARDAWAY: Midsummer Night's. So I'm in that game and Kobe calls me out. I said, Oh, shit, this dude remember me. He remembered that day in Philly and I just didn't take it like he did, obviously, but all he needs is a little something to just get that momentum going. "I'm getting you back. You didn't believe in me, you didn't know me," and we went at each other in the Magic game. Obviously, he was a young pup, I got the best of him in that game, but he did come to me and go, "You know, I want to learn. I want to be the greatest," and I knew then, though, that he was just going to be unstoppable and unbelievable moving forward. But, yeah, that's my Kobe story right there.

MATT BARNES: I love it. He looks for little shit like that. Little chips, something to add to his—

STEPHEN JACKSON: Anything!

ISAIAH THOMAS

Kobe, he was everything to my life. Not just hoop: I wanted to be him. I knew I wasn't just 'cause I wasn't going to be six-six. I wasn't going to be as big as him. He inspired me in so many different ways. Then, when I was able to reach that level of one of the top guys in the NBA, I was able to build a relationship with Kobe, and it wasn't just no hoop relationship. It was an everyday lifestyle relationship. In terms of, if I was going through something, I can hit him and he was hitting me right back. He meant everything to me. When I was able to build that friendship with him, it was crazy, checking my phone and seeing the texts from Kobe. It didn't make no sense 'cause, you know, I looked up to him for so long . . . I can't thank him enough for not just changing my basketball career but changing my way of life.

PHIL HANDY

PHIL HANDY: His realness, man. He was misunderstood, man. I asked him one time, I asked him, I said, "Man, why are you such an asshole?" I asked him that. And he said, "You really want to know?" You know how he was.

MATT BARNES: Mm-hmm.

PHIL HANDY: And he said to me, "I feel, man, some of my teammates don't understand the work." He says, "So I see dudes walk into practice ten minutes before practice and they leave right after. Why the fuck am I going to pass them the basketball? I don't respect their work ethic. I'm in here busting my ass every day, trying to perfect my craft, and these dudes don't want to work on their game. I don't trust them. So I'm not going to pass them the basketball. I'ma ride them hard every day."

DOC RIVERS

MATT BARNES: I remember we were fortunate enough to get one of Kobe's last interviews and he said that series right there to him was the series that always haunted him, that would make him sick. The fact that you guys handled him like that to win the championship.

DOC RIVERS: Yeah, I remember talking to him right after the game and he's crying. He's got tears in his eyes and I could feel his energy. Like, literally feel it. I told a couple of guys after the game, and it was not an energy of sadness. It was an energy that was "I'm going to get you guys."

MATT BARNES: "I'm gonna see you. I'm gonna see you." That was his whole goal.

GLENN ANTON "DOC" RIVERS has been in and around the NBA for over forty years. A thirteen-year pro, he transitioned to coaching shortly after retirement and led the Celtics to a championship in 2008.

DOC RIVERS: It was not a . . . I told a couple of our guys, I said that was not a "Well, we lost." It was . . .

MATT BARNES: I'm going to see you motherfuckers . . .

DOC RIVERS: "I'm going to see you again. I'm going to Goddamn destroy you."

MATT BARNES: Yeah.

DOC RIVERS: You can feel it. You can feel it.

THE GAME

THE GAME: Under these glasses, if I say his name too much, I'm going to start crying, because it's like you would've never thought in a million years that Kobe would meet an untimely demise.

STEPHEN JACKSON: He's a superhero.

CARON BUTLER

All he talked about was the game. I started watching film with him on every plane trip. Just analyzing the rotations, the schemes, the double teams, where they was coming from, how to manipulate the defense. I learned a whole bunch from the Bean. And also, too, when you talk about life after basketball, he gave me a jewel that stuck with me. "The roar of the crowd is not for you, it's for what you can do. And as soon as you can't do it, they'll be cheering for someone else. So work on your second act while you're in the midst of your first."

That's why I started calling him the Remix of MJ because to me, he look like MJ. You sound like MJ. You move like MJ. He's the next best thing. —JALEN ROSE

DE'AARON FOX

Man, Kobe was big. And the craziest thing is, one night in Portland, I was able to sit with Kob' in a library for three hours. It was me, him, and maybe four other people. And I was able to sit with him for about three, four hours, man. It was probably 11:00 p.m. to 3:00 a.m., just sitting in there talking, man. And that's something that kind of . . . I mean, it sat with me most, obviously, when he passed away because this is something that, literally, a year and a half before it happened, I was able to have a sit-down with Kob'. I actually didn't even tell my brother about it and he's a big Kobe fan, but that's something that I'm extremely, extremely grateful for. You know what I mean? Everybody don't get that. Some people might get a picture or an autograph, one little conversation. Just being able to be there after Kob' was done, it was going into my second year and, man, that's something I always think about. What if that didn't happen? Now, obviously, the Kobe thing hit me even harder because I was able to actually have this personal interaction with him.

DE'AARON FOX is a seven-year pro currently playing for the Sacramento Kings. He's known as one of the fastest players in the league.

JALEN ROSE

To me, to watch him from, like, '96 when he got drafted and wasn't even appreciated by his own teammates until that moment where Shaq ended up being the force first forty-six minutes of the game. And he ended up being the last two. And that's why I started calling him the Remix of MJ because to me he look like MJ. You sound like MJ. You move like MJ. He's the next best thing. Made perfect sense. When he really broke it down as to why he is the way he is with certain dudes, I was just like, "Man, I respect that, bro."

JALEN ROSE is a cultural icon. From The Fab Five to Reggie Miller's running mate to sports media royalty, J Rose has been a fixture in the sports world for thirty years. Most impressively, he claims to be the first person with the name Jalen, which has become incredibly common.

ICE CUBE

I was just on Kobe, even though we had Shaq, I'm just locked in on Kobe and just see-ing his progression as a pro, and I'm yelling at Del Harris, "Put him in. Put in Kobe. Put in . . ." I'm yelling, you know what I'm saying? Because Del Harris would just keep this kid on a bench all game. "I'm like, Damn, man. Come on, Naked Gun. You know what I'm saying? Come on, Naked Gun. Get him in there."

TRACY McGRADY

TRACY McGRADY: We were both Adidas guys and both made the jump from high school to the pros. There was an opportunity for me to go out there and just be around Kobe and LA. I stayed with him in the house with him and his parents. Mom used to fry up that fried chicken for us and macaroni and cheese. I would eat good at that boy's house, man. They had everything. He had chores and everything, but . . .

MATT BARNES: Yeah, shout out, Pam.

TRACY McGRADY: Yeah.

MATT BARNES: She was out there cooking. Hell, yeah.

TRACY McGRADY: Absolutely. But to be around Kobe at nineteen years old, bro, you would've thought Kobe had been here before and been around the greats of the game because

his mindset was so different than I'd ever seen in anybody at nineteen years old. This man really and truly thought he was better than Michael Jordan, thought he was going to be better than Michael Jordan.

STEPHEN JACKSON: Thank you, T-Mac.

TRACY McGRADY: You know what I'm saying? At the time, I'm looking at my dog, and I'm like, "You crazy as hell, bro." I'm like, "Bro, something is wrong with you, player," like, "Son, you crazy." We used to watch his homegrown movies, *Come Fly with Me* [and] *Playground*. We used to watch that religiously, bro. Pause it, then might do something, pause, rewind, mimic it. I was like, "Dog." He was obsessed with this shit, karate flicks. I mean, man, he was different, bro. His work ethic, everything just rubbed off on me and how he handled himself, man. Partying wasn't his thing.

STEPHEN JACKSON: Not at all.

TRACY McGRADY: He wasn't trying to hang out. No. "Oh, you going to the club? Ah, shit, I'm going to go to the gym put up these shots." That's what he was about. He was different. Our relationship started to go like this because he was concentrating on trying to win championships, and he sacrificed everything. He cut everybody off to win championships and be great as he possibly could be. I was over here trying to win scoring titles.

GARY PAYTON

He kept asking me stuff every time he played me. I posted him up and I got it. He would always come over to me and sneak in my ear. "OG, man, why you keep killing me on these post-ups, man? You've got to teach me that. What should I do?"

That was just a big thing for me to hear that and to respect that. I couldn't do nothing but respect it and teach him the game because I know I'm a lot older than him and

I was going to be leaving the game soon. I wanted to see somebody in the game that imitates the things that I do and can be dominant at it. This kid was one of them guys. I taught him everything that I knew. We used to stay after practice in LA, and I used to teach him the post-up game. Then he used to fade away. He took it all. We used to do drills about defense. I used to get him, and I used to throw a tennis ball back and forth, and he used to catch it with one hand, catch it with one hand and slide. That's how I learned. And he got so good at it where he used to guard all the top guys.

> That was a good block, young fella, but the play continues. —KOBE BRYANT TO JOHN WALL

JOHN WALL

So, one time, I get Kobe in the post, I'm guarding him in the post, he spins, I block his shot, then Kobe and I chase after it. Think I'm about to get the loose ball and they kick it to him and I run back over there, he shoots a three. And he was like, "That was a good block, young fella, but the play continues." I should've never said nothing because he ended up scoring, like, 20 straight on us. And I was like, You know what, I'm just going to mind my business and not say nothing no more.

CARMELO ANTHONY

CARMELO ANTHONY: He wanted to see if I really was like that. He wanted to see if I was going to fold or if I was going to stand tall. And the minute that I stood tall, he hits me. I'm cracking him back. You know what I'm saying? Hit me again, I'm cracking him back. He falls, I'm stepping over him. "Get up." So then he like, "Oh, I see. Oh, you a bully." That's when he started calling me a bully at that point in time.

STEPHEN JACKSON: He respected that, though.

CARMELO ANTHONY: Oh, he respected that.

STEPHEN JACKSON: No question.

CARMELO ANTHONY: He respected that.

MATT BARNES: He just has a weird way of getting into it though.

CARMELO ANTHONY is one of the best pure scorers ever. Over his nineteen-year career, he won an NCAA championship as a freshman at Syracuse University, made ten NBA All-Star games, and played in four Olympics.

CARMELO ANTHONY: Yeah, man. He had a weird way of just . . . he had a weird way of just be like, "Yo, you nice."

STEPHEN JACKSON: Yeah, he ain't going to say that. Nah.

CARMELO ANTHONY: No, hell no. Hell no.

MATT BARNES: He might not ever even say that. Period.

PAUL PIERCE

PAUL PIERCE: I got my nickname after a Laker game matching up with Kobe. That pretty much cemented my legacy.

MATT BARNES: Going through him.

PAUL PIERCE: Playing against him. He meant so much to me in the basketball world, and just to see him be gone like that, it's like you almost lost a family member.

MATT BARNES: You did.

PAUL PIERCE: I've lost family members, I've lost friends and stuff, but for some reason this one hit. One of the hardest-hitting ones.

STEPHEN JACKSON: He was untouchable, like damn near untouchable to us.

PAUL PIERCE: Yeah, right?

STEPHEN JACKSON: Anything can happen but it can't happen to Kobe.

MATT BARNES: It's not supposed to happen to Kobe, right.

PAUL PIERCE: Right, and so even today, man, I'm just looking at the mural, it's hard, it's hard man.

THE GAME

I still feel indebted to Kobe just for his contribution to the city, for him never wavering from playing for the Lakers. Never being traded, never abandoning the ship. Just taking it into the last game. Oh, my God. I said that, yo, I watched it. I watched niggas double-team. It wasn't easy. I watched him get 60 on the way out. And it's like when we talk about Kobe, I mean, under these glasses, if I say his name too much, I'm going to start crying, because you would've never thought in a million years that Kobe would meet an untimely demise.

JEANIE BUSS

JEANIE BUSS: I'm glad the way you said that we all lost Kobe because when people would say to me and express their condolences, I would correct them and say, "Hey, the world lost somebody really special." And just him as a friend and as a motivator and watching him as a father and a husband, he was a leader and he's irreplaceable. And

the knowledge that he shared with people. I had no idea until after he passed that, I mean, I knew he helped basketball players.

MATT BARNES: He helped everybody.

JEANIE BUSS: He helped everybody, people in every kind of sport and even me, when I think back to after my father passed away in 2013, he invited me to have lunch. And I met him down in Orange County and he brought Gianna with him and he said, "I hope it's okay with you. I brought Gianna because I want her to see—"

MATT BARNES: A strong woman.

JEANIE BUSS: "—a really powerful woman." And I realized later that really what he was doing was motivating me.

MATT BARNES: Absolutely.

JEANIE BUSS: And he was somebody that I valued and will continue to value and I hope that what he stood for and the lessons that he taught people like me, I will continue to pass on to other people. And I think his legend will continue to grow.

JEANIE BUSS is the controlling owner and president of the Los Angeles Lakers. Buss began her career at nineteen as general manager of World Team Tennis' Los Angeles Strings.

It was awesome to see him really give all he had to his girl, to his young daughter, right? And those girls. I seen it in his eyes. Like, "Hey, Kobe, you like this? You having a good time in retirement?" And I could just see it in his eyes that he loved it and he gave it all to them. —JR RIDER

STEVE NASH

You know, when I got to play with Kobe . . . We both got hurt, but having to share the locker room with them at the end of our career, it was an eye-opener in a sense. Because you forget, we got drafted together. We played against each other our whole careers. I thought of him as a competitor. I thought of him as the competition, predominantly. So when I came to the Lakers and you could see the worship that young players had for him, it was an eye-opener because I never had that perspective of him. But that's exactly how I was with Jordan when I came in the league. So I'd been there. I'd done what they were doing to Kobe. How exciting it was to play with Kobe, I'd done having the chance to play against Jordan.

ZACH LaVINE

Kob' was my biggest inspiration. Wearing number eight and things like that, that's one of the main reasons I wear it.

LIL WAYNE

He's a mind state. Kobe is a mind state.

CHANDLER PARSONS

CHANDLER PARSONS: So I got a good Kobe story. My rookie year we're playing here in Staples Center and Kevin McHale pulls me aside. "You're going to see crazy people. You're going to see celebrities there. Lock in on Kobe. He's going to try and bust your ass. He's going to be offended you're guarding him."

MATT BARNES: Absolutely.

CHANDLER PARSONS: I'm like, "Cool. I love it. I'm flattered to guard him." So I go there. First of all, I'm just looking at the court side. My head's on a swivel because I've never seen this before. I'm like, Goddamn, this is crazy. Denzel's there, and this chick's there. I'm like, Wow. So I'm already distracted. And of course I'm starting on Kobe. And Jordan Hill that year had got traded from Houston to LA. So I had known him as a little side note.

And fourth quarter comes around and Kobe looks at me and he's like, "Are you guys staying the night tonight?"

And I'm like looking at McHale, make sure he is not looking at me. I'm like, "Yeah, what up?" I'm like, Ohhh, he's doing it. He's Mr. Miyagi-ing me right now. He's doing it. I'm like, "Yeah, what's up? We're staying."

He goes, "Oh, I'll set you up. I'll get your number from J-Chill if you want to go out tonight." I'm like, Stop. I know what you're doing. Come on. McHale's over there grilling me. "Stop talking to this motherfucker." So I go, he ends up just going off. He has 40 in that game. We lose. After the game right there in L.A. Live, we go to Katsuya. And we're with all the OGs. We're with Camby and they're all taking me out.

ZACH LAVINE is a two-time NBA All-Star and two-time NBA Slam Dunk champion who starred at UCLA before being selected by the Minnesota Timberwolves. He won a gold medal in the 2020 Olympics as a member of the U.S. Men's National Team.

CHANDLER PARSONS was the first Florida Gator to win SEC Player of the Year. He played nine seasons in the NBA with the Rockets, Grizzlies, Mavericks, and Hawks.

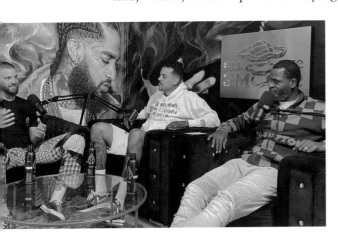

I get a text and he goes, "You're all set at Supper Club—Mamba." And I'm, like, looking around, all right, who's fucking with me? No way. Courtney Lee is my guy. I'm showing him. Is this real?

And I write back. I said something like "Are you coming?" He's like, "No, I can't make it. But my guy will hit you up."

Got the next text from a different number. "Hey, you're set up. Let me know what you need at Supper Club, whatever." So, at this point, I'm telling the table. I'm like, "Guys, I got you. Kobe is my guy. He set it up. Let's go." J. B. Bickerstaff is there. I'm bringing coaches. I'm bringing trainers. I got it. And we have a blast. We have the craziest night ever. Supper Club was the club where the tables were beds. It was awesome. It was nuts. And 2:00 a.m. rolls around and I'm with these guys who made hundreds of millions of dollars. And this waitress beelines right to me with a check. And I'm like, Oh, shit. And my dad's my financial advisor at the time. He would be on my ass if I value-sized my combo meal at Chick-fil-A. And she's bringing me this bill for God knows how much. And I'm like, Oh, man. I open it and it's, like, $22,000. And now at this point I'm sick. I'm physically like, No, no. I can't do that, because the card's going to bounce.

And I'll never forget this chick looks at me, hands me a pen, and says, "Sign for Mr. Bryant." And I'm like, What? I videoed the whole thing. I'm like, Stop. I signed Kobe Bryant on a $22,000 club bill. And everyone, by the way, they say he's tough. He's going to go at you. I'm like, "Nah, this dude was cool as fuck."

STEPHEN JACKSON: That's a dope story.

SHAQ

I got a mural of Kobe and my sister in the house so I see him every day, but it's hard. It just puts me in that "I should've" mode and you should never be in "I should've" mode. So my advice to everybody out there, if you want to get something done, you want to call somebody, you want to say something to somebody, just do it. Doesn't matter if you have past differences, past beef. If you got respect for that person, you love them and you just hadn't talked to him for a while. Get it.

ZACH RANDOLPH

ZACH RANDOLPH: My daughter, she loved Kobe, man. I called Kobe. I got ahold of him when we was moving out here. She was like, "Daddy, I want to play for Kobe." She came to me about it. You know I'ma do anything for my kids.

ZACH RANDOLPH optimized grit and toughness over his seventeen-year career. Z-Bo scored over 18,000 points and was the face of the Grizzlies' "Grit 'n' Grind" era, in which they made the playoffs seven consecutive times.

STEPHEN JACKSON: Yes, that's right.

ZACH RANDOLPH: So I ain't have Kobe's number. I reached out to somebody who did, and, man, Kobe texted me the next day, like, "What's up, Z-Bo?"

I'm like, "Man, my daughter, we moving out there, she want to play. Can she try out? You got a spot for her?" He was like, "She can come. We can see how it goes." I think one of the bigs was hurt or something or just left, moved somewhere. And we came, and it was like the missing piece. Kobe loved her, man. When he told me that he loved my baby, bruh, I told him, I said, "Man, I love you." I said, "You love mine, I love you."

MATT BARNES: Straight up.

> When he told me that he loved my baby, bruh, I told him, I said, "Man, I love you." I said, "You love mine, I love you." —ZACH RANDOLPH

MAGIC JOHNSON

Oh, special, special on the court, special off the court. Kobe changed the game, man. Kobe changed Los Angeles, the NBA. He would work out with anybody. High school, young lady, young man . . . he loved the game. We all love him. He was 24/7 involved. So we miss him even today.

MJ 6

he was unlike

For me, he's the greatest player to
ever play the game. —STEVE NASH

any other player

STEVE NASH

STEVE NASH: For me, he's the greatest player to ever play the game. And he was my hero as a kid. Got a chance to play against him. '96/'97, I came in the league, and that was around the time—

MATT BARNES: Right in the midst.

STEVE NASH: Right. I think *The Last Dance* was '97/'98, so my second year in the league. I mean, you guys remember what it was. We didn't have so much access back then to every single thing on Instagram or YouTube, let alone watching games live. So, you know, MJ was must-see TV. Like, anytime he was on TV, it was must-see.

MATT BARNES: WGN.

STEVE NASH: Yeah, exactly. He just had this charisma on top of all the gifts and skills and, mentally, you know how great he is. Playing against him, the one thing that I think that he was unlike any other player I've ever played against is that there was a real fear playing against him. I've never seen the league be kind of fearful of a player, or have that much reverence for a player, no matter who has come since then. You know, that was a different feeling when you're playing Mike, because you just knew there was such a seriousness, a competitiveness and fire in him. And there was a fear with how that was going to manifest itself potentially on any given night. So he was . . . I mean, where do you want to start and where do you want to finish with him? He was everything.

KEVIN GARNETT

KEVIN GARNETT: JR is having a good game. JR and Mike kind of had . . .

STEPHEN JACKSON: JR Rider.

KEVIN GARNETT: Yeah, JR Rider, shout out to JR Rider.

MATT BARNES: Shout out to Easy Rider.

KEVIN GARNETT: So as we come out of the time-out, just I'm on, y'all, I can't even explain it, I was just like, "Yo, JR, keep killing that nigga. Yo, you killing that nigga. Boning him. Yo, straight up, you're having a good game, y'all keep doing that." But it was on some, like, just fly-by, like he was like, "Yeah, you too."

So as I'm saying that, the nigga right here, Mike can hear me, but I ain't really, I don't really give a fuck, so I double back like, "Yeah, man, you keep killing that nigga. Yo, you killing that motherfucker." So as I say that, I feel it. Hands on hips, legs locked—

MATT BARNES: Good luck.

KEVIN GARNETT : I can't even really describe the next, like, six to seven minutes of play. In this next six to seven minutes of play, y'all, we get two, not one, two ten-second calls, you know when you're bringing the ball up—

MATT BARNES: You couldn't even get it across half-court.

KEVIN GARNETT: You've got to get it across half-court, two ten-second calls. We down 25 now. Mike had 18, he had like 40 now. JR, myself, we ain't scored in, like, about four minutes. Then I subbed out with three other starters. It got bad quick, yo.

So I was like, "JR, my bad, my bad dog. Sorry, man. I'm sorry." He was like, "It's cool, man. I told you just shut your ass up."

JR RIDER

JR RIDER: Hey, that was spot-on, man. I saw that, I was laughing so hard. And that was so real. I had to guard that man, so KG was just on one, feeling good. But I do have another story that, to me, I think is cool. So this is my first time playing

ISAIAH RIDER, also known as **JR RIDER**, is a former NBA player known for his high-flying dunks and scoring ability. He played for several teams during his career, including the Minnesota Timberwolves and the Los Angeles Lakers, and was the 1994 NBA Slam Dunk Contest champion.

against Mike, right? So we go out to center court. They're about to do jump ball. We go out right beside each other, that was my first time playing against the Bulls. And they was like rock stars. Mike looked at my head, looked at the wristband, looked down at me, I had on my own shoes. I had Sky Riders. He looked down on my shoes, looked back up at me.

STEPHEN JACKSON: He just sized you up.

JR RIDER: He did, but, in my mind I'm like, Oh, he probably think I'm trying to look like him.

STEPHEN JACKSON: Yeah.

ISIAH THOMAS

ISIAH THOMAS: I'll never forget, every time Chicago played, Joe Dumars and I would be on the phone and we'd be talking because we got to play against them. And they were playing New Jersey in Chicago. And Joe and I, we're talking, and Jordan came down on the left side, went through a couple of dribbles, and then he took off on the left box and dude floated all the way to the right box. And then laid it up on the other side. And I swear to God, Joe and I were on the phone and for about five minutes, man, it was just dead silence. Dead silence.

MATT BARNES: The fuck did we just see?

ISIAH THOMAS: Yeah. And then all of a sudden it was like, "Hey man, I'll see you at practice tomorrow."

MATT BARNES: Seen enough.

STEPHEN JACKSON: This is what we got to deal with.

ISIAH THOMAS: That dude jumped from the left box and was up in the air and went all the way over to the right box.

WOOD HARRIS

WOOD HARRIS: If you haven't been looking, go look at Michael Jordan's footage, whether you like basketball, go look at Michael Jordan's footage . . . Because Michael Jordan—

MATT BARNES: First step.

WOOD HARRIS: It is so inspiring to see him, because it's all work. That shit is work. That's work.

SHERWIN DAVID "WOOD" HARRIS is a legendary actor who starred in *Above the Rim* as Motaw and *The Wire* as Avon Barksdale.

KOBE BRYANT

MATT BARNES: Have you ever sat down and had like a real off-the-camera conversation with MJ?

KOBE BRYANT: Oh, yeah.

STEPHEN JACKSON: Wow.

MATT BARNES: What is that like?

STEPHEN JACKSON: Looking in the mirror?

KOBE BRYANT: No, it's fun. I mean, it's fun. No, we're really different. It's crazy, like he'll compete—

STEPHEN JACKSON: To you. To you, y'all different.

KOBE BRYANT: I mean, I guess. I mean, he'll compete with any and everything. I won't, I only compete with things that I really am good at. Like I'm not just going to—

MATT BARNES: Compete on something you don't know.

KOBE BRYANT: Yeah, I'm not going to do that.

MATT BARNES: He'll compete regardless.

KOBE BRYANT: He'll compete at everything. He'll talk basketball all day long and not stop: "Well, what would have happened if my '91 against your '03?"

MATT BARNES: What would happen in your opinion?

STEPHEN JACKSON: Come on. We can't ask him that, man.

MATT BARNES: I want to know, would it have been complete dominance, would it have been a seven-game series? What would it have been?

KOBE BRYANT: Well, what he started the conversation with was, well, "I would have destroyed you." I just said, "Listen, just remember who you're talking to." He just started laughing and he's like, "I'm just messing with you. I'm just messing with you." Then we just kind of moved on.

MATT BARNES: That's dope.

KOBE BRYANT: But it would've been fun.

TRACY McGRADY

STEPHEN JACKSON: How was it like playing against MJ your rookie year?

TRACY McGRADY: Shaking in my boots. Shaking the first time I had to guard him. Like, yo . . . Man, first of all, let me go back. 1997. MJ and them made the playoffs, I think they played against the Hawks, right? I'm at the playoff game. Bro, I got an opportunity to go in the back by the locker room after the game. So I'm standing back there. I'm seventeen years old, kid. I've never been around NBA players like this or even I've never been around somebody like MJ. I'm standing back there, kid, and—

STEPHEN JACKSON: Black Jesus.

TRACY McGRADY: Pip comes out, all these players start coming out. Mike comes around that corner, bro, I ain't going to lie to you, the man had a glow, bro. I swear my . . . Dog, that shit is real. I'm not joking, bro. It's real.

TRACY McGRADY, a.k.a. T-MAC is a seven-time All-Star, seven-time All-NBA selection, and two-time scoring champion. He's regarded as one of the best scorers ever and was inducted into the Basketball Hall of Fame in 2017.

I ain't going to lie to you, the man had a glow, bro. —TRACY McGRADY

STEPHEN JACKSON: It's Black Jesus, man. I'm telling you.

TRACY McGRADY: Mike came out, I was like, "Damn, bro." I didn't know what to say, man. I was like, "That's MJ, dog. That's MJ." So, fast-forward, I'm on the court with him my rookie year, it took me about a quarter to get over the fact that this is Mike. Right? But, man, that mystique wears off if you're around somebody for a long time, it wears off. It's like, Okay, shit, let's get it. I damn near had my best game as a rookie playing against him. I almost had a triple double in front of 30,000. We played in the SkyDome.

STEPHEN JACKSON: Yeah, yeah.

TRACY McGRADY: 30,000. Mike had them coming in there, bro. And that was the year they had what? 72 and 10?

STEPHEN JACKSON: In Toronto.

TRACY McGRADY: We was one of them 10.

STEPHEN JACKSON: Yeah. In Toronto.

MATT BARNES: That's what's up. Hell yeah.

JAYSON TATUM

Growing up, my dad, it was all MJ highlights. He was like, "I know you love Kobe, but Kobe got all of this from Mike." He used to show me Mike highlights all the time. I always understood, like, No, Mike the greatest. He the GOAT for the reason.

> [My Dad] was like, "I know you love Kobe, but Kobe got all of this from Mike." —JAYSON TATUM

MUGGSY BOGUES

Well, MJ, he always like . . . well, I'm going to say, he always like to fuck with me. Just that's who we are with one another when we come in contact. I mean, even off the court to this day, walking around, he'll put his hand up high, trying to get me to give him a high five. I'll put my hand down low, you come down and give me a low five. It is just really competing against one another.

MAGIC JOHNSON

MAGIC JOHNSON: I get a chance to represent the country and play on the Dream Team. Play with Michael, make a pass to him, make a pass to Larry Bird, Charles Barkley, Scottie

Pippen, Patrick Ewing, David Robinson, Clyde Drexler, Chris Mullin, Stockton. So it was really amazing for me to be able to be on that team and just crush everybody by over 42 points a game. And I think it opened the game up to all the international players. It became a global game after that. So it was a true blessing. And also, too, it helped me understand that I was going to be here a long time.

STEPHEN JACKSON: Yeah.

MATT BARNES: What were those practices like? I mean, you hear, you see docu-series and docs, they say that's when you handed the torch over to Mike, because I'm sure you guys got more out of the practices than you guys were actually playing.

MAGIC JOHNSON: You're right. We practiced, man, when you got ten egos out on that court like that—

MATT BARNES: Best in the world.

EARVIN "MAGIC" JOHNSON JR. is an entrepreneur and one of the greatest basketball players of all time. He led the Los Angeles Lakers to five NBA championships, and after his playing days he shifted his greatness to the business world.

MAGIC JOHNSON: Yes, going at each other every single day. So one game he decides to say, "Okay, the East versus the West." So, all the East guys, Jordan, Pippen, Bird, Barkley, and Ewing, bam. And then, all the West guys, Malone, Robinson, Drexler, Mullin, and Stockton, so we all played against each other. So Charles Barkley took Malone one time and he scored. I said, "Come on, Karl, you got to get his ass back, so get out on that block and get him back." So I threw it to him and he scored. They come back,

they scored, we scored. So we were all talking smack. So finally we got on a little run, so we scored about eight in a row and they didn't score. Time-out. So Michael walking back, and I don't usually talk trash but I had to that time. So I said, "Michael, if you don't turn into Air Jordan, we're going to blow y'all out." Man, he starts sweating. That tongue went long. You know when that tongue come out.

MATT BARNES: It's over, it's a problem.

MAGIC JOHNSON: He about to do something. Boy, that dude came out after that time-out and he scored about four straight threes.

I said "Michael, if you don't turn into Air Jordan, we're going to blow y'all out." Man, he starts sweating. That tongue went long. You know when the tongue comes out . . . —MAGIC JOHNSON

MATT BARNES: Ooh.

MAGIC JOHNSON : Ooh, ooh. And I went, "Oh, man," then he came down. I got to show you this one. So he stole the basketball, comes down the right side, he takes off, David Robinson coming this way. So Mike just cuffed and he just looked at him.

STEPHEN JACKSON: In the air?

MAGIC JOHNSON: And he kept looking, he kept looking, he kept looking. He went all the way down, Jack. He did a 360.

STEPHEN JACKSON: Ooooh.

MAGIC JOHNSON: Bam.

MATT BARNES: And dunked.

MAGIC JOHNSON: I said, "That's it, that's it, it's over now, it's over now." So he just looked at me, too, to let me know.

STEPHEN JACKSON: Yeah.

MATT BARNES: I'm coming.

STEPHEN JACKSON: It's your fault.

MAGIC JOHNSON: You know who got me to do this? You.

COMMON

MATT BARNES: Most people didn't know you were a ball boy for the Bulls. Is that before MJ got there? Was there any crossover with MJ?

COMMON: Yeah. I was right there when MJ came up. I started a year before.

MATT BARNES: How old were you at this time?

COMMON: I was eleven or twelve. See, my father played in the ABA for a couple of years.

MATT BARNES: Yeah. Mm-hmm. Rest in peace.

COMMON: Yeah, God bless his soul. Thank you, brother. Rod Thorn was one of his teammates. Rod Thorn was the general manager for the Bulls. He said, "Yo, you write a letter, you pretty much get the job." So I wrote the letter and I got the

LONNIE RASHID LYNN, a.k.a. **COMMON**, is a rapper, actor, and activist. Over his storied career he's won three Grammys, an Academy Award, an Emmy, and a Golden Globe.

job. I was there when Mike first came. They all used to give away gym shoes after a few games. I used to get the shoes. I'd be selling them, giving them to my teachers. I had a pair of Air Jordans, some of the first Jordans, and he signed them. I gave them to my father. But my father started wearing them. He was wearing them to my shows. I'm like, "Yo, Pops, you got to put them Jordans away. Jesus Christ, these ain't meant to be worn." It was an incredible experience. I was just geeked to be around all that, be there when Mike first came. I remember Mike had a radio and was playing Houdini when he first came at one of the first exhibition games. They was like, "Nah, you can't play that music." Then, after that first game, man, he can play whatever he wanted.

MATT BARNES: Really? Mike? That's crazy.

COMMON: Yeah. Mike. They was like, "Oh. We good. Yeah. We good."

MATT BARNES: You can play whatever you want. Any cool one-on-one interactions you had with him at a young age you can recall?

COMMON: Just shooting around with him. Well, one thing happened where these kids asked me to get an autograph and I was like, "Okay, I'll do it for five dollars." I went and took it down to Mike. I said, "Yo, can you get this autographed?" He told me to sign it. He was like, "Naw, you sign it. I don't need to sign it." So I signed it and took it up to the kids. And the kid looked

and was like, "Man, this ain't Michael," because I spelled Michael wrong and shit. He was like, "Man, what the hell?" So obviously I didn't get my five dollars. Even later, as I said, I had hoop dreams. Y'all know that. I saw Mike. I played in one of those celebrity games. I thought I did good. Mike saw me and was like, "Man, you better stick to rapping and acting." I was like, "Man. This guy."

MATT BARNES: Oh. MJ is classic.

SHERYL SWOOPES

MJ, he was my dude. I was going to be in front of the TV. Anytime MJ was on TV, I was like, "I got to watch. I got to watch." It was something about . . . And it wasn't me watching, because I wanted to be like him. In my opinion, nobody will ever be like him. But there was something about the way he played the game, and how competitive he was, and how tough he was, and how he walked out there and was like the name of your show. It was like, "You all don't want none of this." I saw that in him, and I was like, Damn! I want to be that way. I want to be good enough where when I walk out on the court, I feel that confidence, and people, my competition. will see me and they're like, Damn! Here comes Sheryl today.

> In my opinion, nobody will ever be like him.
> —SHERYL SWOOPES

MICHAEL RAPAPORT

He was on that shit. And people go, Oh, he was a fucking asshole. I'm like, Yo, you think, anybody that's transcendent, Marlon Brando, he was a notorious piece of shit to work with. Not knowing his lines, showing up crazy. James Brown, fucking shitting on the band. Anybody that's transcendent. Denzel Washington, he's supposed to be a motherfucker on set, but look what you get. You're not going to get that. And I'm sure when people, like anybody that's that fucking sick, of course he was a motherfucker. We're not playing, this is the NBA. He's coming to fucking bust your fucking ass. And if you don't like it and you're too soft, then get the fuck up out of here.

MICHAEL RAPAPORT began his acting career in the '90s with his first role on the TV show *China Beach*. He was featured on several hit TV shows in the '90s like *NYPD Blue* and *Friends*. He's acted in more than fifty films since 1992.

Of course he was a motherfucker. We're not playing, this is the NBA. He's coming to fucking bust your fucking ass. And if you don't like it and you're too soft, then get the fuck up out of here. —MICHAEL RAPAPORT

STEVE KERR

MATT BARNES: What was it like—I mean, I'm sure this is a common question—playing with Mike? We heard you guys had your differences at times. But just overall, him as a teammate? Him as a competitor? Is there a friendship there?

STEVE KERR: There's a mutual respect that exists. We don't really stay in touch, but we see each other maybe once or twice a year. Whether it's at a game in Charlotte, or All-Star Weekend. Or maybe a golf tournament or something in Lake Tahoe. We just seem to run into each other once in a while because we're traveling the same circuit. It's always a great reunion. It's so much fun to relive those days, and to ask about our teammates, and talk about the good times back then. Being his teammate was hard. He was really tough on everybody, because his whole philosophy was he had to toughen us up to get us ready for the playoffs, and the finals. He came after us, and you had to stand up to him. You had to survive the MJ test. The guys who survived it, he had immense respect for them. People know about the fight that we got into together. That was just about him testing me. Probably the best thing I ever did was not take his crap and sit back up. He respected it, and we got along ever since, so it's all good.

CHARLES OAKLEY

We ate a lot of McDonald's back then. MJ ate McDonald's every morning for breakfast. Every morning he ate McDonald's.

CHARLES OAKLEY is regarded as one of the toughest players ever. Over his nineteen-year career, he was the muscle for the Chicago Bulls and then the New York Knicks, where he made an All-Star Game and was selected to two All-Defensive teams.

You had to survive the MJ test. The guys who survived it, he had immense respect for them. —STEVE KERR

RIP HAMILTON

So Allan Houston was killing me. Like I said, he killed me my first two years, right? So when MJ came third year now, and I feel like I'm growing up, you know what I mean? I grew some hair on my chest, like I've been through the war and the battles a little bit. So I got *big bro*. Like I got the bully in the room, right? So I'm a little bit more confident. So we playing against New York, we're playing against New York in Washington, and first half I go out and I give Allan Houston 30 in a half. Right? I'm like, Okay, for all the times this motherfucker been killing me and getting me a foul trouble, I'm in his ass right now. You know what I mean? So we in halftime, we talking, coach talks, does a speech. MJ come up to me. He was like, "Hey, man, hey, young fella, you had a great half, but big bro going to take over the second half so don't worry about it."

RICHARD CLAY "RIP" HAMILTON was a star shooting guard in the NBA for fourteen years. He won a championship with the Detroit Pistons in 2004 and won a NCAA championship in 1999 with the UConn Huskies.

JAYSON TATUM

JAYSON TATUM: I've got a funny story. We was in Paris, and I met MJ earlier in the morning. And then that night we had a dinner, so it was like Melo was there, Blake was there, Russ, Spike Lee. Everybody was there. I remember, I'm still nervous. I walk in, MJ is sitting down, his wife is next to him, and Spike next to her. I walk in and I was like, "I'm going to go say what's up to them before I sit down." I talked to him earlier, like we had a whole conversation. I kind of know him. But then I walk over to him and my hands start sweating. And I was like, "What's up, Mike?" And when I went to shake his hand, I knocked over his wine glass on the table, and it broke. And I was—

MATT BARNES: Oh, shit. Damn.

JAYSON TATUM: I was like, "Oh. Let me get a napkin. Let me help you out." He was like, "Young fella, it's cool. It's good. You're all right." I turned around like, Yo. I'm tripping.

MATT BARNES: The fuck did I just do?

STEPHEN JACKSON: MJ, man.

VINCE CARTER

MATT BARNES: So 2003, you're the leading vote getter in the league, MJ's last year. You decide to give MJ your starting spot. Talk to us about that.

VINCE CARTER: So basically, yeah, I decided to, but it was encouraged by the league that it was a good idea. All the powers that be said that it was probably a good idea that MJ starts in his last All-Star Game. I'm not a fool. You know what I'm say-ing? Yeah. I am not a fool. First of all, we all look up to MJ and he's a hero and that's a memory that nobody else can talk about.

STEPHEN JACKSON: Black Jesus.

VINCE CARTER: That can't be duplicated. But I got a story, I could tell this story forever. So I pulled him aside, but it was all day in the morning practice, or shooting around or whatever you want to call it. I was like, "MJ, take it."

"No, you earned this whatever."

"All right, cool. I am not about to argue with you."

So we get down there, right before we run it out I say, "MJ, take the spot. You going to start." I said, "If you don't take the spot, I'm going to stay in the back. And I am not going to come out." I said, "I'm not getting blackballed from the league because you talking about this, you earned it. Yeah. Okay, cool. I earned it. We know that. But you start."

VINCE CARTER, a.k.a. HALF-MAN HALF-AMAZING, holds the NBA record for most seasons played at twenty-two. Over the course of his more than two-decade-long career, Carter made eight All-Star games and scored over 25,000 points. He's regarded as the best dunker in NBA history, and his performance at the 2000 Slam Dunk Contest was one of the biggest pop culture moments the NBA has ever seen.

MATT BARNES: You going to get this.

VINCE CARTER: Right before they called him for the starting lineup. He still wouldn't go. You see at the last minute, it's where he took his . . . if you see it, the last minute he take his shirt off and he go out there, but he would not go out. I was like, "Please, please just go, because I'm going to walk to the back." And it isn't happening so—

MATT BARNES: Fuck it.

VINCE CARTER: He takes it and I was like, "Man, thank God."

Cannabis

7

roll another

MATT/STAK

MATT BARNES: Did we actually get in trouble together our first time, Jack, in Golden State in '07?

STEPHEN JACKSON: Yeah, because you had me drinking that liquid shit and had me thinking it was going to give me a passed test and I failed.

MATT BARNES: Well, that's because you smoked all . . . I mean, the liquid could only do so much. You smoked the whole motherfucking pound, thinking the drink is going to flush your system. You can't blame that part on me.

SNOOP DOGG

MATT BARNES: The night we beat Dallas and we ended up at your hotel at the Ritz. You remember that?

SNOOP DOGG: Boy, do I ever.

MATT BARNES: That shit was crazy.

SNOOP DOGG: We had some strong conversations that night.

STEPHEN JACKSON: Hold on. But let me tell you how this started. You sitting at a desk with a 50 box of Swishers. We were on Swishers then.

SNOOP DOGG: Oh, yeah.

STEPHEN JACKSON: You had a 50 box. You busted down, roll it, hit it, passed it to him, and then we go around. Roll another. You did it for about an hour and a half.

MATT BARNES: We was double fisting.

STEPHEN JACKSON: And we didn't move.

MATT BARNES: My sister was so high. My sister didn't smoke. She was so high, she passed out. Remember, we was watching—

SNOOP DOGG: Yeah, Sis was in there.

MATT BARNES: You had the blue carpet treatment cartoons.

SNOOP DOGG: My movie.

STEPHEN JACKSON: What did the hotel people do?

MATT BARNES: Bro, so the hotel people come banging on the door and we as athletes, we're like, "Fuck."

STEPHEN JACKSON: We're nervous.

MATT BARNES: I mean, we are still in season, so we think like, Aw shit, here we go. They come in, "Hey, Snoop, good game fellas." They unscrew the windows, lift the windows up just so the smoke can go out, ask us we need anything, and leave.

STEPHEN JACKSON: We all look like, Is this real?

MATT BARNES: What the fuck?

SNOOP DOGG: Yeah, VIP. That's when Stern was the president.

STEPHEN JACKSON: Five-star hotel, man. They come and open windows.

SNOOP DOGG: Me and Stern had an understanding.

CALVIN CORDOZAR BROADUS JR., a.k.a. **SNOOP DOGG**, is one of the biggest icons in music history. He was a pioneer for the West Coast hip-hop movement in the '90s, and today is one of the most brilliant marketers and businessmen in the game. Snoop was the first guest in **ALL THE SMOKE** history to openly smoke weed on camera. That decision sparked quite the conversation with Viacom executives, but it was agreed that there's nothing illegal about smoking some weed in California! Shout-out to Snoop for opening that door.

KEVIN DURANT

KEVIN DURANT: I feel like it shouldn't even be a huge topic around it anymore. Is it great? Is it good for you? Can it help? Is it bad? But when everybody on my team drinks coffee every day and taking caffeine every day or guys go out to have wine after games or to have a little drinking here and there. Marijuana should be in that tone, why are we even talking about it? It shouldn't even be a conversation now. So hopefully we can get past that and the stigma around it and know that has done nothing but—

MATT BARNES: Make people have a good time.

KEVIN DURANT: —make people have a good time, make people hungry, make people just come together. That plant brings us all together.

KEVIN DURANT is one of the best scorers to ever grace the earth. He's scored 28,000 points and counting and has four scoring titles under his belt. Outside of hoops, KD is one of the more accomplished athlete-turned-entrepreneurs.

That plant brings us all together. —KEVIN DURANT

DWYANE WADE

DWYANE WADE: I want to vibe with Barack, especially drinking wine.

MATT BARNES: I want to smoke a joint with Barack.

STEPHEN JACKSON: Me too.

DWYANE WADE: Yeah, me too. Yeah, I want to vibe with Barack.

MATT BARNES: Okay, did you say smoking a joint, or drinking wine?

DWYANE WADE: Oh, both. We can do it.

MATT BARNES: Yes.

ALLEN IVERSON

ALLEN IVERSON: I'm smoking, I'm up the—

STEPHEN JACKSON: You was all in back then.

ALLEN IVERSON: Yeah.

STEPHEN JACKSON: Yeah, you was all in.

ALLEN IVERSON: Man, I'm smoking whatever. And Coach Thompson came up there and it was Coach Thompson looking at me. Man, I remember just trying to get myself together. Went, washed my face. Just trying to get right.

MATT BARNES: You can't wash the high off.

STEPHEN JACKSON: You can't, it doesn't work.

ALLEN IVERSON: No, but he didn't know. He didn't know.

STEPHEN JACKSON: You think he didn't know, he knew.

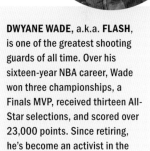

DWYANE WADE, a.k.a. **FLASH**, is one of the greatest shooting guards of all time. Over his sixteen-year NBA career, Wade won three championships, a Finals MVP, received thirteen All-Star selections, and scored over 23,000 points. Since retiring, he's become an activist in the LGBTQ+ space.

ALLEN IVERSON: He probably knew.

STEPHEN JACKSON: Yeah, man. Come on, you know he knew that, bro.

ALLEN IVERSON: I came in one day, he was like, "You all right, little man?" "Yeah." I was trying to get away from him so fast. Like, "I'm cool, Coach." He told me, "Why are you standing so far back there? Come here." Now, you telling me, he probably knew.

STEPHEN JACKSON: I'm telling you, he did. Come on, man.

ALLEN IVERSON: He probably knew, this little motherfucker high as hell.

> I came in one day, he was like, "You all right, little man?" "Yeah." I was trying to get away from him so fast. Like, "I'm cool, Coach." . . . He probably knew, this little motherfucker high as hell. —ALLEN IVERSON

STEVE KERR

Well, it's funny, because I spoke out about this a couple years ago. I had my own health issues, with my back surgery that went wrong. I was getting prescribed all these opioids constantly for pain. I'd read about this stuff. I'm like, I'm not taking this stuff. This Oxycontin, or Vicodin, or whatever. It just seemed so insane.

KEVIN GARNETT

MATT BARNES: What do you think about now with the narrative finally shifting about cannabis? And what about your thoughts about cannabis and sports?

KEVIN GARNETT: I think education, man. I think when it comes to cannabis, people have to understand that, I think they see cannabis in a recreational use, and the education has to come out about the healing parts—

MATT BARNES: The benefits.

KEVIN GARNETT: —of it and the benefits of it. I think as a society, meaning that it's a more older society thinking of the ways of recreation, it's more millennials and younger kids that's really exposing and giving us education on the benefits. And I think our society's changing and I think everybody's starting to see this, more importantly, the benefits. I think the sooner they get CBDs into sports, I think we'll start to see a bigger change. You guys don't know that we probably take about six to seven pills a night before we play.

MATT BARNES: No clue.

KEVIN GARNETT: And that's just to be able to step on the court. You got inosine, you got Vicodin, you got two Tylenol, you got two Advils. The kidney is only supposed to be able to process so much. If we're not hydrating and bringing in liquids and fluids and draining that, your liver's catching all that, your kidneys are catching all that.

GARY PAYTON

MATT BARNES: I know you've teamed up with my homeboy Burner. Shout-out Cookies and came up with a GP strand.

STEPHEN JACKSON: Hold on. Hold on. Tell him the story. Tell him the story first.

GARY PAYTON: I'm going to tell him the real story.

STEPHEN JACKSON: Tell him the story. Everybody that don't know, this is the real story about the Gary Payton kush.

MATT BARNES: I want to hear.

STEPHEN JACKSON: Everybody around the world. They all talking about "I need Gary Payton. That's all I need. That's my favorite." Everybody's screaming for that right now, and you all don't even know how the OG found out about it. Go ahead and tell them, OG.

GARY PAYTON: It's all good. One day I was just sleeping, and Stak hit me on the phone. He was hitting me a bunch of times, right? So I was like, Damn. I hope ain't nothing wrong. So I picked up the phone and he was like, "OG, you know I came to the Bay to pick up some of your stuff." I said, "Some of my what?" He was like, "The Gary Payton." I said, "Man, I don't know nothing about no weed." He said, "You don't know about no strand of the weed they got on you?" I was like, "No." He was like, "Man, OG man, you'd better look into that."

You know the reason that strand is really hot is because of you all giving me the props as the OG. Everybody fucks with me, so I appreciate all of you, all and everybody in the world who get down with me. Plus the weed is bomb and fire.

STEPHEN JACKSON: That shit is awesome. Oh my God.

ISIAH THOMAS

ISIAH THOMAS: I'm in the champagne space and I'm in the cannabis space and my kids love it.

STEPHEN JACKSON: I know that's right.

MATT BARNES: Hey, Dad is the plug.

STEPHEN JACKSON: Dad is popping.

MATT BARNES: Dad is the plug.

ISIAH THOMAS: My kids love it.

STEPHEN JACKSON: That's dope.

AL HARRINGTON

AL HARRINGTON: That's the first time I smoked, it was in Phoenix.

STEPHEN JACKSON: Yeah, because I remember you smoked and you had the drug test the next day and you passed it.

AL HARRINGTON: It was in Phoenix. I didn't pass it. I diluted it.

STEPHEN JACKSON: You diluted it.

AL HARRINGTON: 'Cause what happened was y'all told me, 'cause the trainer called me on the way to the gym. He was like, "Yo, you gotta piss this [week]." I'm like . . . Get the fuck outta here.

MATT BARNES: First time he ever smoked.

AL HARRINGTON: First time I ever smoked.

STEPHEN JACKSON: Everyone came to my room.

AL HARRINGTON: I got off the bus, he told me, I got off the bus and I went to Whole Foods and I got that Sonne's #7 thing y'all told me to get. I got that. I drank it. That shit was disgusting.

STEPHEN JACKSON: Word.

AL HARRINGTON: And I just started pissing all day. So I got to the game and I'm nervous so I don't piss when I get there. I tell them I can't piss after the game. So you remember what y'all was waiting on me and everything and when I pissed it was just all water. So that's when I realized you get a dilute test.

STEPHEN JACKSON: You get one.

AL HARRINGTON: You get one. So that was my one. That's how I passed. It was all water. He put the thing in. He was like, "This is all water." And I was like, "What you want me to do?"

MATT BARNES: I'm a fucking athlete. What you mean?

AL HARRINGTON: I'm hydrated. But y'all got me through that. I remember that nightmare. I was paranoid in that room, man.

PAUL PIERCE

The more and more you learn about it, and learn how it can help you . . . Right now we're in the middle of an opioid crisis, where people are getting addicted and dying. If you have alternate ways of medication such as cannabis, why is there a big deal surrounding it? We don't look at alcohol the same way. The stuff that's really killing you, we don't frown upon, but we're frowning upon cannabis. You know, hard alcohol brands are sponsoring professional teams. Like you said, motherfucking Celtics smoking cigarettes in the locker room, how many people do those take down a year? The real problems, they don't look at. But I think because cannabis has been stereotyped as a Black drug for such a long time, that people realize, it's no color, everybody partakes. And like you said, I think the key is education.

Right now we're in the middle of an opioid crisis, where people are getting addicted and dying. If you have alternate ways of medication such as cannabis, why is there a big deal surrounding it? —PAUL PIERCE

JOHN SALLEY

JOHN SALLEY: My first time smoking weed was in Sacramento, obviously.

MATT BARNES: Surprise. Surprise.

JOHN SALLEY: It was the first time I slept eight hours, too, and I got up and it was . . .

MATT BARNES: You tried that year?

JOHN SALLEY: That's the year. Yeah. My senior year. My last year. My senior year. I was a senior citizen. My last year . . . I remember I got on the bus with five minutes to go without a jersey and just a sweat top on and they were like, "Yo. What's up, vet?" I went to my teammate, and when he gave it to me, he was like, "Sal, this the chronic now."

MATT BARNES: Mm-hmm.

JOHN SALLEY: I was like, "Man, give me that." Man, my left leg became my right leg and I was feeling on myself. I was outside doing yoga. I was bending backwards. I was like, "Man, if I had this from the beginning in the NBA."

JOHN SALLEY was a key member of the iconic "Bad Boys" Pistons teams. In his later years, he played for the 72–10 Bulls and the 1999–2000 Lakers. After his playing days, Salley had a very successful media career.

SNOOP DOGG

SNOOP DOGG: I'm so happy for the awareness of cannabis and how it's becoming so necessary, so relevant. The topic of discussion, so many bars, dispensaries. So many states, cities, so many politicians. It's like a great discussion. It's great for health benefits, it's saving a lot of people. It's keeping people here, it's keeping our sanity level right.

STEPHEN JACKSON: Preach!

SNOOP DOGG: But I would like to see all of my niggas that's locked up for weed to be released ASAP, right now.

DRAYMOND GREEN

Well, I think when you start to really do the research and look at all the things, the one thing I do know is all these painkillers that they give us to get through the season, listen. It ain't it. They give us all these anti-inflammatories. People get Toradol shots. If there's a shot that can make you feel nothing for six to eight hours. Completely fucked-up and go play in a whole game and not feel it. And by the way, after that motherfucker wore off and you feel like you got hit by a truck the next day. That thing can't be good for me. I look at it like, after all the research that's been done, it's not legalized in, I don't know, maybe over half the states. I don't know the numbers, I don't study it. But if you're going to continue to give guys Toradol shots and anti-inflammatories, something got to give because it has been proven to not be as bad as that. And that is one thing I know for sure.

The one thing I do know is all these painkillers that they give us to get through the season, listen. It ain't it. —DRAYMOND GREEN

STEVE NASH

STEVE NASH: You know what, I was never really a smoker, but the indica has really helped me sleep. I don't know if you guys use indica for sleep, but . . .

MATT BARNES: I use it for life.

STEVE NASH: Yeah. That, man. I wasn't aware of it during my career, but sleeping was always a problem for me, and it's the number one way to recover. I really wish it could have helped me perform to have that sleep agent that isn't as kind of gnarly as the sleep pills that I refuse to take. The proof's in the pudding, right? It's becoming legalized, so we know enough, we're educated enough now to know that it's not like the stigma that needs to follow it around. There are so many purposes and packages that allow it to help many, many people. So I think it's just one of those parts of evolution in society that we're gaining, and I think within time it'll be a much more mainstream and common thing in all walks of life, especially those of professional athletes.

CALVIN JOHNSON

I didn't realize until I got to the NFL. Well, I don't understand, when I'm in college, you don't really suffer the same injuries that we did when we got to the pros. For some reason, you still have maybe a little bit more bend and elasticity to your joints and stuff, I guess, when you're in college. But when I got to the league, man, those hits and stuff, they started to compound and take their toll. And so literally, I

CALVIN JOHNSON, a.k.a. MEGATRON, was a game-changing wide receiver. Johnson made six Pro Bowls and was inducted into the Pro Football Hall of Fame in 2021.

would say, probably my first two years in, I started probably to have a good routine after the game. Sometimes after practice. I'm getting it in. It's the only thing that brought comfort, that would allow me, one, to sleep. Allow me to relax and allow me to focus in and free up some creativity as well. There's so many different things that you can use it for. You say inflammation, that was the key for me. But really just the overall emotional feeling of well-being that I got when I would indulge, especially when you're dealing with pain.

> It's the only thing that brought comfort, that would allow me, one, to sleep. Allow me to relax and allow me to focus in and free up some creativity as well. —CALVIN JOHNSON

BARON DAVIS

BARON DAVIS: Cannabis is probably a thing that should be passed, right? I love the way that the NBA has adopted it. I feel like it's better than drinking. You know what I'm saying?

MATT BARNES: Pills?

BARON DAVIS: Yeah. People taking pills and all that. And it's like, you can manage somebody who smokes a lot of weed. You know what I'm saying? You can have a conversation with somebody, probably a long conversation—

MATT BARNES: Too long.

BARON DAVIS: It's known to be a healing agent and have all these kinds of nutrients that our bodies need. The reason why we

BARON DAVIS, a.k.a. **B-DIDDY**, brought his LA swagger all the way to the league. He was the star player of the 2006–07 "We Believe" Warriors team with Matt and Stak. Davis was selected to two All-Star games over his thirteen-year career.

was blowing and smoking, you know what I mean? After the games was like, shit, man, we smoke and watch the game, drink a gallon of water, man, we used to drink a gallon of water and be like, "All right, bro, I'm going to be all right."

STEPHEN JACKSON: We just smoked and watched film.

BARON DAVIS: Eight dudes in a row. We go to my spot or your spot. And we'll sit there and smoke and watch.

RICKY WILLIAMS

I think if I was smoking more earlier in my career, I think I could have avoided a lot of these injuries because when I started smoking, I didn't get hurt anymore.

ZACH RANDOLPH

It's good for your bones, man. It's medicine. Like you said, you ain't got to take all them pills, mess your stomach up, and be fucked-up later on in life. And I'd rather smoke than drink anyway.

STEPHEN JACKSON

What was your first impression of the Spurs when you got there? Because, when Pop told me he wanted to sign me, the first thing he told me, "Look, I know you smoke weed, we're going to sign you, but you can't smoke weed." And you know me: "Sure, Pop. I'm not going to smoke ever again in life." Smoked a couple hours later.

SUE BIRD

SUE BIRD: So it's just CBD to me personally. I'm obsessed. This summer we didn't have drug testing in the bubble so it was a totally different experience. I slept amazing the whole season. You know what I mean? I was literally taking the gummies the second the games were over because I was like, All right, I'll probably be back in the hotel in like an hour and a half. This will hit at the right time. Because, as you know, sometimes

SUE BIRD is one of the greatest women's basketball players of all time. She won four WNBA championships, two NCAA championships, and five Olympic gold medals.

it's hard to sleep after games. So, yeah, to me it's been life-changing as an athlete. And I think the THC part of it for people who smoke or whatever, I don't see that being any different from like I said, all the drugs that have been pushed for all these years.

MATT BARNES: Jack, it sounds like she might need to come to a smoke-out when she retires. We'll teach her how to roll some joints and enjoy the other side of it as well.

STEPHEN JACKSON: I would be honored. I would be honored.

SUE BIRD: My smoke team.

KENDRICK PERKINS

KENDRICK PERKINS: Ah, shit. Jack. Look, you know me. Goddammit, man. Shit. You know I used to be with the motherfucking loud. You know, I want the purp, right? As long as you don't pass me no wet blunt, we cool. Right? So, shit. I'm smoking that loud, doing what I do, right? I'm doing it the first year doing TV. I go on *Undisputed*. Now, mind you, I smoked the night before. But I'm in Cali. You know that Cali weed hit it a little different.

STEPHEN JACKSON: It's different. It's different.

KENDRICK PERKINS: I hit the motherfucking loud, man. And shit. I went on *Undisputed* with Skip and Shannon. And right then, I'm still kind of blowed the next morning. And I forgot every motherfucking thing I was going to say. I said, you know what, let me chill right now, because I'm trying to start my new career. Because, look, some people . . . some people could smoke loud and focus. I'm not one of them dudes, dog. That put me over the edge. So I say, you know what? Let me take a break from this, man. Let me really lock in. But, hey, look, to every motherfucker out there who is smoking loud, smoke it. Fire up one for me. I'm just one that can't handle it and go on TV and talk about it the next morning because I still be blowed.

MATT BARNES: You got to know yourself, that's the most important part about being a smoker. You got to know yourself.

RON ARTEST

MATT BARNES: So the Lakers won a championship this year in honor of our brother Kobe. Obviously rest in peace. I read somewhere or saw somewhere, you say you smoked ten blunts and partied like you was on the squad?

RON ARTEST: Let me tell you why I said that.

MATT BARNES: Let me tell you why.

RON ARTEST: Because we've been through so much with this marijuana thing. Outside, we got to put the weed down back in the days people went to jail for marijuana. So I'm like, I really appreciate the movement of cannabis. I appreciate the movement. And I prefer not to speak on it. I prefer not to smoke on shows like this, but I respect what people are doing. So I support, you know what I mean?

METTA SANDIFORD-ARTEST, previously **METTA WORLD PEACE**, played seventeen years in the NBA with a stacked résumé. A 2010 champion, 2004 Defensive Player of the Year, and four-time All-Defensive selection, Sandiford-Artest represented Queens, New York, to the fullest.

MATT BARNES: Has it helped you at all with, like you said, the mental health, mental focus, any of that?

RON ARTEST: I like CBD. I don't like the THC as much because the THC, for me, it takes you out of your mind a little bit. I smoke THC sometimes. But CBD, I like it better. Because if you're working every day in the office, you don't want to be on THC all the time. So I like now they have options and you see like Viola has options in different levels for your mood. And the CBD products are amazing. The whole thing is great. I think it's great. Some people don't. I think it's great. So that was all that was honestly, I didn't have ten blunts. I have like one or two.

MATT BARNES: Happy for them to win.

STEPHEN JACKSON: I had the other eight, probably.

RASHEED WALLACE

RASHEED WALLACE: This is back when Seattle Sonics had a professional team. So Portland was only two hours away. So coach let us ride back. Those who wanted to drive back, they let 'em ride on your own.

STEPHEN JACKSON: Like we did when we played Sac.

RASHEED WALLACE: So it's me, Damon, and he got his homie driving. So we boom, boom, boom, and banged a J, banged a J. I banged a J, he banged a J, and boom, that's it. So we're riding down, enjoying music, talking shit. And he told him, slow down a little bit, but at that same time, that's when the cop nabbed us. So he had us out there for a while. He was like, "Man, I smelled the marijuana. Where's the drugs?" Like, "Hey, dog, we ain't got nothing. You're late. If you would've popped us maybe fifteen, twenty minutes ago, you could have . . . But we have nothing. You're late." So he brought the dogs out, he brought two, three more cruisers out. Who rides by us?

MATT BARNES: The team bus.

RASHEED WALLACE: The fucking team bus, dog.

RASHEED WALLACE, a.k.a. **SHEED**, brought that Philly energy to the University of North Carolina, Chapel Hill, and then to the NBA, where he played sixteen years and won a championship with the Pistons in 2004. Sheed is one of the original stretch big men and was also a pioneer for the timeless Nike Air Force 1 sneaker.

Welcome to the Big Leagues

8

nobody can

back you down

DeMAR DeROZAN

STEPHEN JACKSON: What was your "Welcome to the NBA" moment?

DeMAR DeROZAN: Shit, I had a lot of those. Shit, man, I remember playing against Brandon Roy.

MATT BARNES: People don't know how nice Brandon Roy was.

DeMAR DeROZAN: Listen, I tell everybody that stuff. It was Brandon Roy, and the way he did it was so effortless. I didn't even exist on the court.

MATT BARNES: Smooth.

DeMAR DeROZAN: It was the most disrespectful shit I ever encountered. For years, it made me so upset that he did me like that, but that was him. You know what I mean? I always wondered, man, people don't know how Brandon Roy really was, man. He was a problem, he was a problem. You know what I mean? He welcomed me to the league, for real.

Compton's finest, **DeMAR DeROZAN** is a six-time NBA All-Star and has been named to the All-NBA Team three times. DeRozan spent nine seasons with the Toronto Raptors, where he made significant contributions to the team's success, including five playoff runs.

MATT BARNES

STEPHEN JACKSON

DEMAR DEROZAN

SNOOP DOGG

STEPHEN JACKSON: You got a lot of movies. You play yourself a lot, but you are in a lot of movies. *Starsky & Hutch*, which is one of my favorite movies. I laugh at that shit so much. Half baked.

SNOOP DOGG: You know that nigga really hit me in real life in *Starsky & Hutch*? I'm going to take you to the scene. It was the golf course scene. Me and Vince Vaughn. We were rehearsing, and the scene that says Vince is going to say a line and then Snoop's character, Huggy Bear, is going to interrupt him and Vince is going to say, "Hey, don't you interrupt me!" Okay, me and the director, Todd Phillips, we get an understanding so it's time to shoot. Nigga like, "And action!" Nigga saying his lines, I'm all ready and doing my shit. The nigga say something. I'm like, "Hey, man." That nigga said—*he slapped the dog shit out of me.*

STEPHEN JACKSON: No way!

He slapped the dog shit out of me. —SNOOP DOGG

SNOOP DOGG: Nigga, on my mama. He slapped the dog shit out of me. The nigga in me was going to punch him, but the actor in me . . .

STEPHEN JACKSON: You sold it! You sold it!

SNOOP DOGG: The actor in me was like, "Ahem." I shrugged it off and I went into my next line and I did that shit and I killed that shit nigga. They was like, "And cut." Everybody started clapping and the nigga Vince Vaughn hugged me tight as a motherfucker and said, "Man, don't kill me, man. I just felt the urge, man." I said, "You felt the urge? You dog head motherfucker, you."

JOE JOHNSON

JOE JOHNSON: My "Welcome to the NBA" moment? Was playing against . . . my rookie year was MJ's first year back in the NBA with the Wizards.

STEPHEN JACKSON: Ooh.

JOE JOHNSON: Yeah, we played against them in the fourth game of the season. I was starting. Eric Williams get hurt in the second game of the season, small forward, so they start me, and I got to guard MJ. Paul Pierce like, "Man, I'ma get him in the fourth quarter. I need you to get him the first three." I'm like . . . Look, I'm like, "All right. All right, bet." Man, we got out there, first off, 'Toine [Antoine Walker] and MJ talking

JOE JOHNSON, a.k.a. **ISO JOE**, played eighteen years in the NBA with seven All-Star Game selections. He scored over 20,000 points and is tied for second for most game-winning buzzer beaters ever.

stuff to each other on the tip, you know what I'm saying? So MJ tell Paul, "I got to come all the way back to the NBA just to get a pickup game with you, just to get a run with you." So they all going back and forth the whole game. But I'm like, "Man, y'all

MATT BARNES

STEPHEN JACKSON

JOE JOHNSON

got to chill." You know what I'm saying? I'm the one got to guard this man. But it was a fun moment, man. I embraced the challenge, and I had so much fun. But I got so many pictures and memories from that moment. And even the video, it was crazy. It was on TNT. I'll never forget it.

CJ McCOLLUM

CJ McCOLLUM: Shit, I had a couple, man. Jamal Crawford, Lou Williams, Manu Ginobili, Tony Parker too . . . He called [the play] "three fists wedge." They ran a wedge over and over again. I'll give you all three of them. The first time I guarded Jamal Crawford, he had three threes in a row. It was like, bang, bang, bang. I think I fouled him on one of them, "Sub, get out." That was it. First time I played Lou Williams, you watch Lou and you think Lou is nice, whatever, whatever, but I'm just going to guard him, and you can't touch Lou. And he's got the right-to-left crossover pump fake, he's got a right-to-left crossover leaning jumper. He hit me with both. First time, right to left, fade, bang. Second time, pump fake, I jumped, and one. I was like, "Oh, man." "Sub, get him out." Next West Coast road trip, got to play the Spurs next. Welcome to the land of Manu Ginobili. Manu, he starts talking in his language, looks at pop. He holds up like . . . In my mind, he's calling me a loser. He holds this up and I guess it's like angle, like he wanted a screen, a high-angle screen.

STEPHEN JACKSON: Mm-hmm.

CJ McCOLLUM: He backs up to half-court. He throws the ball, runs at me, Euro. They run the same play, seven times in a row. He scores on five or six. And I think on the sixth one, he passed to somebody for three. And that's when I was like, "Damn."

MATT BARNES: This shit is for real.

CJ McCOLLUM burst onto the basketball scene when his Lehigh Mountain Hawks upset Duke in the 2012 NCAA Tournament. McCollum currently plays for the New Orleans Pelicans, and averaged twenty-plus points per game each year from 2015 to 2023.

KEVIN HART

KEVIN HART: The first show was rough. Dude threw a chicken wing at me. This is a true story. Threw a buffalo wing at me.

MATT BARNES: Connected?

KEVIN HART: I'll never forget, sauce and everything. I swear to God, connected, a little sauce got in my eye. At the end of

KEVIN HART is one of the most prolific comedy minds in the game. Hart started his comedy journey performing in male strip clubs, and through hard work and dedication climbed to the top of the ranks. Not only is he a comedian, he's also an award-winning actor, founder, and entrepreneur.

the day, I'm a man. Shut up, bitch. You can hear it in the back, "Fuck off the stage." "Yeah, all right. All right. You all can get hard." Politely put the mic back in the stand and walk off.

UDONIS HASLEM

UDONIS HASLEM: Derrick Coleman, Derrick Coleman.
STEPHEN JACKSON: DC.
UDONIS HASLEM: DC fouled the shit out of me one game when he was playing for Philly, and I say, "Damn, DC, you tried to hit me that hard?" He say, "Young fella, if I tried to hurt you, you would've been on a stretcher."

ISAIAH THOMAS

My "Welcome to the NBA" moment was . . . So the first game of the season we played the Lakers. Kobe Bryant, obviously my favorite player ever. There was a rule in training camp. Paul Westphal, rest in peace, guys would try to back me down and they would just always turn the ball over for whatever reason. I'm not saying I'm a super defender. It's just they were trying to exploit the mismatch, but always seem to turn the ball over and take a bad shot. So in training camp, Paul Westphal was like, "Nobody's backing down I.T. Like, don't do it, or you're getting subbed out." So when Paul Westphal put me in the game, I remember the second quarter, he's naming who everybody got. And then I'm like,

"Coach, who I got?" He's like, "You got Kobe and remember, nobody can back you down." And it was funny. Because I was like, "I appreciate you putting me in, but, bro, Kobe's backing everybody down." It didn't matter. So the first three possessions, they do a little iso. So I'm over behind Kobe, just smiling. I'll smile and try to guard him and knowing he's about to fade away. He hits two out of three shots. The first shot he hit, I'm sprinting downcourt, just laughing, like I'm here. The first time in my life where somebody scored on me, I was smiling and happy about it. Because that was my favorite player, so it was like even touching his jersey. I was like, "Damn, I made it. You can hit this fadeaway on me all day, I'll be solid." That was my "Welcome to the NBA" moment. Paul Westphal throwing me in there and being like, "Nobody can back you down." And me having to guard Kobe the first three possessions of my NBA career.

BARON DAVIS

BARON DAVIS: Probably John Stockton.

STEPHEN JACKSON: He cooked you?

BARON DAVIS: He stole the ball from me.

STEPHEN JACKSON: Oh, he didn't cook you, he just stole the ball from you?

BARON DAVIS: Imagine just getting in the game and you look up trying to get an inbound pass and that shit gone. You think you got to steal and it's like, "Aw, man, I got to steal." And that shit gone. I was only in the game for like . . . I could have played eight minutes that night, but them first two minutes, it was just turnover, turnover, turnover, bucket, and-one, and-one. And I was like, "What the fuck is going on?" Go back in, the same shit. You just couldn't find him, bro. And so it was embarrassing.

MATT BARNES: He one of the smartest.

BARON DAVIS: And then I would say the other one was Stephon Marbury. He was killing us. But I'm a rookie coming off the bench and he did something. He was like, "Yeah, and one." And he looked at me, he was like, "Yeah, you don't want none of this. You can't guard me." And Elden Campbell was like, "Ooh, you going to let him talk to you like that?" So I'm on a bench, hot. I'm on the bench, hot, I'm ready to fight everything. But that was like, he was cooking me too.

JAMAL MURRAY

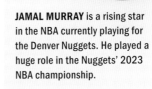

I missed my first seventeen shots, which is almost a record, coming into the league. So five games later, I made a shot. That was kind of a welcome to the NBA. Because that was, like, my first real doubt where I was like, "Damn, nothing is going my way." Not just one or two games, but like, nothing is going down for me. Another time was when Mike Conley whooped me. He had, like, 25 and 15 on splitting pick and rolls and finishing floaters. So I was like, I'm like, "Yeah, I can't hang with this guy." Jrue Holiday picked my pocket seven times in one game. Those were a few of them.

JAMAL MURRAY is a rising star in the NBA currently playing for the Denver Nuggets. He played a huge role in the Nuggets' 2023 NBA championship.

RASHEED WALLACE

MATT BARNES: What was your "Welcome to the NBA" moment?

RASHEED WALLACE: I would have to say, it was my rookie season. We were playing Phoenix. I know you all remember him, Joe Kleine.

MATT BARNES: Redhead.

RASHEED WALLACE: Arkansas.

STEPHEN JACKSON: Oh my God.

RASHEED WALLACE: So we're playing, and you know me back then, I got to dunk, boom. I'm running downcourt. "Hey, you little motherfucker, if you do that again," he said, "I'm going to wipe you out." "Man, whatever dog. You ain't going to do nothing to me."

STEPHEN JACKSON: Strong him up.

RASHEED WALLACE: Two, three plays later, we ran the same play, just a little different option. And I'm trying to go to the rim. I got the ball in my hand. The next thing I know, I'm grabbing for hands, getting up off the floor.

STEPHEN JACKSON: He was a lumberjack or something, dog. He was too strong, dog. For basketball, you didn't need all that.

RASHEED WALLACE: He said, "I told you." He said, "Don't bring that shit down here with me." And I felt as though that was mine.

MATT BARNES: Just a regular foul, no T, no flagrant, no nothing.

JAYSON TATUM

JAYSON TATUM: I remember, the Cavs run on the floor. And then LeBron was the last person in warm-ups. And when he ran on the court, he ran past me. I said, "Damn." I just start getting nervous. I start shaking. The first shot I ever took in the game, I set a screen for Kyrie. I slipped it. Ky threw me a float pass, and I thought I was a wide-open, so I'm like, "I'm fixing to get my first bucket. I'm going to calm down." Man, I tried to lay it up. I don't know where Lebron came from . . . he came, sent that shit to the fifth row. I didn't score until the second half. I didn't get my first bucket until the second half.

STEPHEN JACKSON: Was that your "Welcome to the NBA" moment?

JAYSON TATUM: That was for sure my "Welcome to the NBA" moment. My first shot, LeBron came out of nowhere.

JAYSON TATUM is one of the brightest young stars in the NBA. In his young career, he's already racked up five All-Star selections and five trips to the Eastern Conference Finals. He is the youngest player in Boston Celtics history to score ten thousand points.

PAUL GEORGE

PAUL GEORGE: Well, my real "Welcome to the NBA" moment was the first time I seen Boston play and they had Rondo, Ray, Paul Pierce.

STEPHEN JACKSON: KG.

PAUL GEORGE: KG and Shaq. And all them cats on the floor at the same time and that was like legit my first welcome to the NBA moment right there.

MATT BARNES: He said this is like the Monstars.

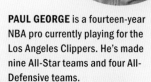

PAUL GEORGE is a fourteen-year NBA pro currently playing for the Los Angeles Clippers. He's made nine All-Star teams and four All-Defensive teams.

PAUL GEORGE: It was like . . . I'm watching from the bench like, Wow. Watching these dudes, idolizing these dudes, and now I'm that close. I was in a suit and shit but in my mind I'm like, I'm that close to getting there. So it was just a dope moment to see and to be able to witness that.

ZACH RANDOLPH

ZACH RANDOLPH: Let me tell you a funny story. I was at the Beverly Wilshire after the season. The trade deadline about to come up. I see Kevin Pritchard, he was the general manager at the time in Portland. So I see Kevin downstairs in the check-in. I'm like, "Kevin, what's up?" He like, "Man, how you doing?" He like, "Man, hey Zach. Man, I'm not trading you, you're good," because I wasn't expecting to see him, he was just down in the lobby. "I'm not trading you, you're good." My first time getting traded, bro. "I'm not trading you, you're good, man, don't worry about it."

So I go upstairs, I tell my brother, I'm like, "Shit, man. I just seen Kevin. I ain't going nowhere. I'm still going to be here." Because obviously I didn't want to get traded. Any player at their first time, some players that's at an elite level can say that, but any of them get traded their first time, it's going to bother you. So I'm like, "What?" So I go back upstairs, I'm giggling. I ain't getting traded. The show come on, first thing they say, "Zach Randolph is going to New York."

MATT BARNES: Same day?

ZACH RANDOLPH: Yeah, I had just seen him. Same day as the draft. I said, "Damn."

MUGGSY BOGUES

My personal "Welcome to the NBA" moment was when Buck Williams gave me eight stitches. I went down and we're playing New Jersey and I'm going down trying to get this little loose rebound in the lane. And he let me know that this is not where I belong. I caught a big elbow right across my eye, had eight stitches from that moment. That was my introduction to NBA.

TYRONE CURTIS "MUGGSY" BOGUES is the shortest player to ever play in the NBA. A Baltimore, Maryland, native, Bogues didn't let his height stop him. Over his fourteen-year career, he racked up over 6,700 assists.

Mentors & Leaders

9

he taught

me everything

ON STEVE SMITH

STEPHEN JACKSON: I was coming off the bench. I was playing well, I was averaging like, shit, 16, 17 off the bench. Pop was starting to play me more and more and more. This is one reason why I love Pop because of the opportunity that he gave me. Pop calls me up to his room. You know this, the principal's office feeling. I had went out the night before and got into some shit with Rashard Lewis. Well we ended up getting into a little fight at the club and it never hit the media. Shout-out to Rashard Lewis. We did some crazy shit that night.

MATT BARNES: That's pre–social media though.

STEPHEN JACKSON: Ayy, pre–social media.

MATT BARNES: '03.

STEPHEN JACKSON: No listen. If social media was there, the shit we did that night. Oh, we was in jail, easy.

MATT BARNES: That's what you're thinking about.

STEPHEN JACKSON: I get to his room, Tim is in there too. So I'm like, Oh, shit. So when I sit down, Pop is like, "You didn't do nothing wrong." Because I'm sitting there like . . .

MATT BARNES: We always feel guilty.

STEPHEN JACKSON: I don't give a fuck. That's just Black man, we feel guilty all the time. Fuck. You know what I mean? Motherfuckers ask me why I don't skate. Because, shit, I've been skating on thin ice my whole life. Pop is like, "Jack, you're all right. You didn't do nothing." He's like, "You've been playing well. I talked to Tim. I think it's time that we start you. We're going to put you in the starting lineup."

MATT BARNES: Who was starting at the time?

STEPHEN JACKSON: Steve Smith. OG, Steve Smith. And at the time he was my big brother. Like he was everything to me on that team. Taught me everything. He showed me how to get loose for the game, how to dress with suits, how to be a professional. Everything about how to pregame, everything. He taught me everything. Him and his wife at the time . . . That was my third year in the league. So him and his wife were like my big brother and big sister. They used to invite me over to cook for me and all kinds of stuff. Make sure I had stuff at the house. When he told me that, I was excited, but my whole time I'm thinking, Damn. How am I going to tell the OG I took his spot? That's not my intention, but I'm just trying to play. I'm just trying to hoop. So when he tells me it's a bittersweet feeling, I'm excited. When I get to the game, I walk in the locker room and I see Steve Smith and our lockers are right by each other all the time. And I'm trying to sneak by him. Because I don't want to address it, you know what I'm saying? He felt it.

MATT BARNES: Right.

STEPHEN JACKSON: Because normally [I'd say], "OG, what's up?" So as I'm sneaking by him, he turned around like "Young fella." As he would call me all the time. "Young fella." This ain't personal between me and you.

MATT BARNES: That's dope.

STEPHEN JACKSON: Go out there, do what you've been doing. This ain't personal between me and you . . . We know what's going on and I'm rooting for you. I'm your biggest fan just like you've been mine. That gave me the feeling like I belong. Okay. You know what I'm saying? Like now I'm going to start.

MATT BARNES: Especially someone like Steve Smith.

STEPHEN JACKSON: Gave me the okay. I belong. He was like, "You've been playing well, you deserve to be starting." That moment. You know what I'm saying? Okay, I belong here.

MATT BARNES: That's what's up.

STEPHEN JACKSON: And I now owe that to Steve Smith.

We know what's going on and I'm rooting for you. I'm your biggest fan just like you've been mine. —STEVE SMITH TO STEPHEN JACKSON

MATT BARNES

So I'm coming into the 2006 season working out for football in the summertime 'cause my brother played football. Still working out basketball but like, Fuck it, I'm going to try to make a jump to the NFL. We had lined up some NFL tryouts for me if this basketball thing didn't work. Then Baron Davis hits me like, "Yo, we got open gym down here in Oakland today if you want to play." I was in Sacramento so I just happened to drive down. Made that little push down to the Bay, played in this open gym. Played well. Not knowing that Nellie was upstairs and watched us. So when we're done, Nel-

lie comes down and puts his arm around me like, "Hey, what do you got going on? Where are you going to camp this year?" I'm like, "Shit, I don't know. I don't have a job." And he's just like, "Okay, well, I can't promise you anything. We've got sixteen guarantees already. We're going to invite a few people to come to camp just to fill out the roster. I can't promise you a spot, but if you play like you play today, I'm going to give you a chance." So I'm like, Okay. This is the first time a coach has had enough time to even talk to me, really recognize me. He just gave me that little bit of confidence that I needed. So I go into camp, do what I got to do. They ended up cutting two dudes and I make the team. So I start off on the bench and kind of work my way into playing and then playing a lot. There was a little run there. I got hot, I had, like, two or three games in a row where I was over 20 if I'm not mis-

taken. And we come down in one city and you know how much Nellie smoked. I didn't have a sweatshirt and it was cold and Nellie tried to get me his dusty-ass jacket that smelled like a pound of motherfucking cigars. I'm like, "I'm cool." But he almost

bullied me into wearing it. So I sat there and just wore his little nasty-ass little smoking jacket. But it was like right there, like this is the first time that a coach is, like, fucking with me and really giving me attention and showing that he believed in me. That little bit of confidence was all I needed.

> So I sat there and just wore [Nelly's] little nasty-ass little smoking jacket. But it was like right there, like this is the first time that a coach is, like, fucking with me and really giving me attention and showing that he believed in me. That little bit of confidence was all I needed. **—MATT BARNES**

KOBE BRYANT

MATT BARNES: What personal growth did you go through from three-peat with Shaq, he's gone, until you won your next title with Pau and the new crew?

KOBE BRYANT: I understand how to connect the team more. I didn't have to with Shaq because Shaq was the guy that connected everybody and still drove a hard bargain, but he was the jovial one and connected everybody. So I figured out how to do that, but do that in my own way.

MATT BARNES: Right.

KOBE BRYANT: You know, with my sarcasm and dry humor or whatever the case may be, and being authentic with guys, but still being able to build that relationship and understanding this is what it's about. As a result, we wound up having the closest team I've ever played on it, man. But that was the biggest change.

STEPH CURRY

STEPH CURRY: Coach Kerr is, he's special, man. He's wise in terms of how to manage people, right? That's a big thing in the league no matter if it's the first guy or the fifteenth guy. You have to be able to be honest, be able to set expectations, and figure out ways to get the best out of guys. I think anybody that would play for him would tell you, you always know where you're at. You always know. If you get a couple DNPs, he's going

to tell you why, and he's going to keep you engaged. He's not just going to walk by you and not say nothing.

STEPHEN JACKSON: He's a great motivator too. I won a championship with him when I was with the Spurs. I remember I used to come out of the games a lot when Pop used to pull me for making mistakes. And I remember in the finals, I didn't start Game 6 off well at all, and Pop kept pulling me. But he kept coming to me. He's like, "You're going to make some big shots. I guarantee you." And he kept telling me that. I was in a funk so I really wasn't hearing him. I end up making three big threes in the championship game to win the championship. He's one of them guys that he's so educated and so smart about the game that he can see shit that you don't even see.

STEPH CURRY: 100 percent. And the cool thing about it too is he's had every seat almost in the NBA.

STEPHEN JACKSON: Yes, and won in every seat.

RENEE MONTGOMERY

The advice Geno Auriemma would always give us was that no one cares. People think that people care about your situation. No one cares. They don't care if we're battling injuries. They don't care if we have no seniors. People never care. And so once you realize that in all aspects of life, your boss don't care what's going on at home. No one cares. And so I've always kept that mentality. People don't care why you're late. You're late. If you keep that mentality that no one cares, figure it out, and do it right, that's what stuck with me.

RENEE MONTGOMERY is a former professional basketball player, sports broadcaster, and activist. She's currently vice president, part-owner, and investor of the Atlanta Dream.

People think that people care about your situation.
No one cares. —GENO AURIEMMA TO RENEE MONTGOMERY

ALLEN IVERSON

I went through it. I went through it. But I remember Coach Thompson. Man, we was playing Villanova, and a dude had a sign that said, "Allen Iverson, the next MJ." And had MJ crossed out and had OJ. And it was four dudes in the stands. And they had on all orange jumpsuits with chains and shackles and all that. And Coach Thompson was like, "Nah. If y'all don't get them out of here, if y'all don't get them out of this gym right now, we are not playing." And they escorted them out of there and the game went on.

ALLEN IVERSON's influence and impact is hard to put into words. AI showed people like Matt and Stak that it was okay to be your true self. Iverson played fourteen years in the league, won an MVP in 2001, and sits at number 28 on the all-time scoring list.

PAUL PIERCE

MATT BARNES: Talk me a little bit about . . . because we were laughing about it on set at ESPN, maybe a month ago, about Club Shiznit.

PAUL PIERCE: Oh, Club Shiznit. Shout-out to Club Shiznit. I had a basement that was like a club, when we didn't have practice the next day we were like, "All right fellas, we're

going to have a good time at my house. I'm going to have a chef come through, we're going to go out, we're going to meet at my house at like 2:00 a.m., we're going to go until about 6:00 a.m."

MATT BARNES: You got to do it.

PAUL PIERCE: All the guys on the team, and we invite girls over, and we go from 2:00 a.m. to 6:00 a.m. And we're like, this is Club Shiznit. You know what I'm saying? We're going to be here from 2:00 a.m. to 6:00 a.m. We're going to have a good time right here, we can't get into any trouble, we're going to be good right here, I'm going to make sure everybody is good, and then, you know, go home. And the players loved that. Perk was talking about it. It was a good time for the fellas, but that's how we built our comradery. So I'd bring in all the young boys, this is how we're going to kick it, and that brought chemistry, you know?

MATT BARNES: Mm-hmm.

STEPHEN JACKSON: 66 wins. God-dammit.

PAUL PIERCE: When GP first got traded to Boston, he did not want to be here. But once he went to Shiznit, he was cool.

SHANNON SHARPE

MATT BARNES: Tell me what it was like playing with one of greatest quarterbacks of all time, John Elway. And he had a cannon too.

SHANNON SHARPE: It was great. It was unbelievable. John was all about respect. You see how some of these guys, when they don't get the ball, they throw the water coolers and they're stomping. He would never show you up. You run the wrong route, you tip a pass and he gets intercepted. He's never going to show you up. If you did something that he didn't agree with, he's going to talk to you on the sideline or he's going to wait till the next day and he will talk to you behind closed doors. That's what I love. He gave me that respect. I mean he didn't have to do that because he was John Elway. He was already an MVP. He was already a Super Bowl champion. So he had already built up his credentials. He showed a young kid respect and so for me, okay, whatever you need.

DWYANE WADE

MATT BARNES: I heard LeBron learned a lot from you.

DWYANE WADE: Yeah.

MATT BARNES: You know as far as how you just gave Shaq credit. As far as approaching the game, and winning, and this, this, and that. LeBron hadn't had that up to that point.

DWYANE WADE: Yeah.

MATT BARNES: So tell me a little bit about that.

DWYANE WADE: Yeah, and I knew that. I knew he was a hell of a player. I think we didn't know how great he was going to be, but we knew greatness was there. He just continued to show us each year what greatness looks like.

MATT BARNES: Mm-hmm.

DWYANE WADE: For me I took it upon myself to try to give him the knowledge, and what I was given from the guys I played with. Meaning what I was given from GP, and Shaq, and just those legends, Zo. I tried to give that same game to 'Bron. We became inseparable in that sense. You know me, because he recognized that in me as well. He respected me enough as a big brother, as well as competitor, that he believed that I'm not going to bullshit him.

MATT BARNES: Mm-hmm.

DWYANE WADE: That I'm giving him real game.

JAMIE FOXX

JAMIE FOXX: *Ray* came along. That movie came along and it was like, I had been preparing myself, not knowing that this movie was going to come up. But when I got with the director, the director was like, you know, when we first started working on *Ray*, first of all, I had to be 157 pounds first day.

MATT BARNES: Yeah. That was a bunch of weight. Yeah.

JAMIE FOXX: Yeah. I'm getting ready to jump up to this Tyson thing. I'm walking around now like 205, but I had to drop to 157 and then he was like, "Okay, I've got a problem. I got to be able to hold the camera on you, but I need somebody to play the piano for you." I said, "No, man, my grandmother taught me how to play the piano when I was five years old. So I'm equipped. I'm ready to go." Now, mind you, nobody was really thinking about the movie *Ray*. We wasn't thinking about that. It was an independent film. And then finally I meet Ray Charles and I had to really win him over. And I said, "Mr. Charles, I just want to do the best that I can to tell your story." And he's like, "You know what, can you play the blues?" So we sat down on the piano and we started playing the blues and everything like that. He moved into the Thelonious Monk, which is real intricate jazz shit. And then I hit a wrong note. He said, "Why the fuck would you do that?" I was like, "I was just trying to keep up." And he said, "That's what life is, taking your time to hit the right notes." So I finally played the piece, right. He got up, slapped his leg, "The kid's got it," and he walked out.

VINCE CARTER

VINCE CARTER: We bring Charles Oakley in, and on my second day of training camp, he puts his arm around me and says, "I got you, I'm going to teach you the league. You listen to me." So what do you say to that?

MATT BARNES: Yes, sir.

VINCE CARTER: Facts. That's what it was.

MATT BARNES: How do you like your coffee?

VINCE CARTER: Carry this bag right here. Carry this bag right there. Oh, okay, cool, I got you. So it was funny, but then back to *The Last Dance* when . . . You remember when they showed Scottie?

MATT BARNES: Fucking up Pip?

VINCE CARTER: Bro, I was like "Oh, snap, you been doing this since '86, my nigga?" Yeah, that was me, that same.

MATT BARNES: That big-ass hand slapping the shit out of people.

VINCE CARTER: It was just funny. So ever since then I was like, "Yo, you all see what happened to Pip right there, that was me bro, that was me." That's what he's been doing forever. It was just cool. I knew I was in good hands, and to this day when I see Oak, bro, he still treats me like a rookie bro. You know how Oak, heavy, old, big—

MATT BARNES: Heavy-hand-ass motherfucker.

VINCE CARTER: Head, yeah, exactly, old alligator hands, just rough like . . . Bro, every time he beat on you I'm like "Bro, I'm not a rookie no more, but what's good, sir? You good? All right, cool," because he made the game easy for me, man. He played with MJ so he got to see his preparation. I played with Doug Christie, who played with

Magic, I played with Dee Brown, who played with Bird. I played with Antonio Davis, who played with Reggie Miller. I had guys on my team that played with greats.

MATT BARNES: Some real vets.

VINCE CARTER: Right. They played with greatness and they taught me how to handle myself with all the attention that was coming in. It made the game easy for me.

CHRIS BOSH

MATT BARNES: How was it, your one year play with VC?

CHRIS BOSH: It was tough. It was tough but he did an awesome job. Looking back on it, he was only like twenty-five years old. And he took me under his wing, he'd take me out to eat on the road. He even came over with dinner with me and my parents. And he showed me things. He took me under his wing. I'm not sure if people knew my capability coming into the league. I had supreme confidence in myself so I knew I could help the team right away. I knew that he wanted to win and so did I. So I always wanted to be that rookie that showed up in the game, you know what I mean? Because there was so much pressure and he was so good.

CHRIS BOSH played thirteen years in the NBA and made eleven All-Star games. Bosh was a part of the Miami Heat Big Three alongside LeBron James and Dwyane Wade, and together they won two championships in 2012 and 2013.

JALEN ROSE

JALEN ROSE: The next year, we were in Game 7 against the Bulls in the Eastern Conference Finals. In that game, fourth quarter, I made two straight shots and they called a time-out. He took me out the game. I was pissed. I was mad. Nobody else in the world, in my mind, even cared. I can't believe this just happened. And I ain't going back in. So for the last five minutes, I'm sitting over there. I can't believe I ain't going back in. I didn't have media responsibilities. They had to go to Reggie. They had to go to Larry. So I ain't even really have to talk to the media. So I basically took a shower pill and jumped on the bus. I was pissed, and I felt like I was going to sit in the back and not talk to the coaching staff. And so I walked up, I was like, Damn, Larry's already on here. I was going to wait for some other people, but I was so early. I was like, Damn, I'm going to just walk past them and not say anything. And he's like, "Jalen!" I turned around like, All right, Coach. He had a beer in his hand. He was like, "I fucked up. I should have got you back out there."

MATT BARNES: That feel good, though? Doesn't help, but it feels good.

STEPHEN JACKSON: Coaches don't do that now.

JALEN ROSE: Never.

STEPHEN JACKSON: Coaches don't do that. They've got too much pride.

JALEN ROSE: Never. I let it go right then. Next year, I was the one that won Most Improved Player. I went from being the sixth, seventh man to in the starting lineup. He did make it up to me. So I'm forever grateful.

KENDRICK PERKINS

STEPHEN JACKSON: What was it like building relationships with Doc Rivers and Paul Pierce?

KENDRICK PERKINS: Paul, he took me under his wing when I got to Boston, I ain't going to lie. Let me tell you what Paul did. Paul is like that guy like us. He wants to see where your heart at. He want to see if you got some, if you're a real one. So my first preseason game ever, I go against the Detroit Pistons. They got Big Ben Wallace. They got motherfucking Derrick Coleman down there. That's my first preseason game. I played like ten minutes. I had eight and eight in that motherfucker. I'm in that bitch dunking, going in, Big Ben shooting that little broke jump hook and shit. So Paul was like, "Hold on, young fella, got some dog in them." And Paul put me through a test one time. He was like, "Yeah, I see you in here. You in here getting early, let me see where

your heart at." He dropped $1,500 on the floor. Now, $1,500 to me at the time, shit, that's a lot of motherfucking money. So it's six, seven inches of snow out there. Paul like, "I bet you won't go outside and give me a hundred push-ups in your tights in the snow." I said, "Shit, you got me fucked-up. I'm going out there and knock these motherfuckers out." Went out there and knocked out one hundred of them. One hundred in the snow with tights on. Came back and got my motherfucking bread. And Paul was like, "Oh, nah, this motherfucker like that. Aye, we keeping you."

UDONIS HASLEM

UDONIS HASLEM: Shout-out to Brian Grant, was probably at that time the closest person to me. He really taught me a lot at that time, about work ethic, the grind in this league, being undersized, shooting that little mid-range jumper, you know what I'm saying? I just thought I was going to get that post work down there at six-seven. That shit wasn't realistic. I had to learn how to shoot that mid-range.

STEPHEN JACKSON: Yeah.

UDONIS HASLEM: Took me out on his boat, man, and really took me under his wing down here. Man showed me a lot of love. Took me out to the strip clubs with him, took care of me. BG took care of me.

UDONIS HASLEM spent his twenty years in the NBA with the Miami Heat and won three championships with them.

MATT BARNES: As he should. Yes, sir.

UDONIS HASLEM: All I had to do was have his coffee for him, he ain't played by his coffee. If you ain't have his coffee, your ass is grass. That's all I had to do was have his coffee.

MATT BARNES: I remember them rookie duties. I don't know if that shit exists anymore, but they really used to have to bring the paper, the coffee, the doughnuts.

UDONIS HASLEM: We had no Uber, dog. We ain't have no Uber.

MATT BARNES: Yeah.

UDONIS HASLEM: Remember that shit? We had to go get your coffee with no Uber.

STEPHEN JACKSON: Yeah. Yeah.

UDONIS HASLEM: Uber, you can press a button and just have a car pick up and take you there. You had to figure that shit out and them vets didn't want to hear that.

MATT BARNES: Yeah.

UDONIS HASLEM: They didn't want to hear, "I couldn't get no car." They ain't want to hear no cab shit. You had to have them people's shit. These guys got Ubers. They could press a button, they go get our shit, and come back quick, whatever we need.

STEPHEN JACKSON: Yeah, right.

UDONIS HASLEM: We ain't have that.

MATT BARNES: Have shit for the plane, have shit after the games, when you hop on that late-night flight, you got to go have the drink ready. Like it was some real rules and regulations that had gone down.

UDONIS HASLEM: Yeah, man. But then at the end of the day, they took care of you.

MATT BARNES: Oh, absolutely.

UDONIS HASLEM: Whatever it is, they took care of you.

MATT BARNES: Per diem.

UDONIS HASLEM: Yeah.

STEPHEN JACKSON: All kinda shit, man.

MATT BARNES: Per diem was everything when I first got in the league, I'm like, "What? What's this?" Like the OG's used to pass the little per diem checks down.

UDONIS HASLEM: Yeah. BMF that shit, boy, blow that shit fast. BMF, that shit ain't last. That per diem they gave us, that per diem they gave us, ain't have no per diem last. That shit burn a hole in our pockets, man. We spend the per diem so fast.

STEVE NASH

STEPHEN JACKSON: You kind of talked about it earlier, but being recruited by one school, going to Santa Clara. Tell me some memories about Santa Clara and being recruited by one school.

STEVE NASH: Yeah. I mean, for me, it was exciting just to have a scholarship offer. That was like my ticket. I wanted to play in the NBA, and I know at the time it probably seemed improbable, but I could kind of see a clear path. I could see that my skill level could get there, and if I could athletically catch up a little bit with my work ethic, I knew that I would put the time in and if I was improving at this rate, in two years, four years, six years, there's no reason why I couldn't kind of rein some of these other players in. And that's kind of the way I went about it. And Santa Clara was an incredible squad, a great coach again. Really tough. Which, he was hard on me, especially when I first got there. And I'll say it was the greatest thing that ever happened to me. I mean he had me thinking about quitting, and going through that experience made everything after that . . . It was easy to overcome adversity, and so I thank him. He gave me mental toughness. As you guys know, like great players in the NBA all have mental toughness, the ability to overcome, to face obstacles and challenges, and more than anything, that's what I got at Santa Clara. Now the experience was great too. Great teammates, still friends with all my teammates. It was a special experience in that respect. But as a basketball player, I learned a lot from the coach, and primarily I learned mental toughness and the ability to just not give in, not fall, not take your foot off the gas no matter how dark it got some days.

WIZ KHALIFA

Best piece of advice Snoop ever gave me was probably just to be myself. Keep doing me. He was like, "You gon' be around." And he refers to himself as Snoop Dogg. He's like, "You gon' chill around Snoop Dogg. Don't be like Snoop Dogg. Be like Wiz, nigga. I love you because you Wiz. You a motherfucking rock star. You work hard, you do this, you do that. You fuck with this audience, you fuck with that audience." He's like, "Always keep that. Never change it. Never give it up."

Best piece of advice Snoop ever gave me was probably just to be myself. Keep doing me. He was like, "You gon' chill around Snoop Dogg. Don't be like Snoop Dogg. Be like Wiz, nigga. I love you because you Wiz." —WIZ KHALIFA

ICE CUBE

ICE CUBE: Sir James moves down the street from me and his cousin is Dr. Dre. And so he's the only one on our street with turntables. This is Jinks turntables with . . . He'd bring the cardboard outside. He's spinning on his head and shit. And we went down the street looking like, What's up with this dude? We didn't know about breaking and all that shit, but he was graffiti. He just was a B-boy. He was the hip-hop guru on the streets. So I started to go down there and hang with him because I used to go out with his sister. So I would just go to hang with him.

O'SHEA JACKSON, a.k.a. ICE CUBE, is a rapper, songwriter, actor, and film producer. He was a pioneer of gangsta rap in the late '80s with N.W.A. and continued his success after music in film and business. He's currently leading Big3, a basketball league that has helped countless retired players.

MATT BARNES: What age was this?

ICE CUBE: Thirteen, fourteen, fifteen. And people would trip. They'd be like, "Man, why are you going out to hang with that weirdo, man?" I'd be like, "Man, that sucker be doing some dope shit in that room, man." And so I started rhyming and me and him, we'd just started working. He would put on beats. He would help me while I'm on beat because I didn't have any beats. I was just a cappella, you know what I'm saying? So he helped me. And then Dre came through one day and heard me rhyme. And Dre kind of took me under his wing because him and Jinks . . . Jinks would always want to compete with him. Jinks would say, "I'm better DJ than you, nigga. I'm better. I do better beats. I do better everything." And Dre was like, "Come on, man. Start me out with that." But I would be more helpful, you know what I'm saying? I was like, "What y'all working on as the *Wreckin' Crew*?" You know what I'm saying? And like, "Let me write something for you." You know what I'm saying? I was trying to get in. And I wrote some for him and it was a hit. We wrote it together, me and Dre. And it was a hit and they had slowed-down hits, like "Turn Off the Lights" and shit. But this was actually a hit that was moving, that they was playing all day on the radio, so. He trusted me.

CHARLES BARKLEY

CHARLES BARKLEY: I'm a rookie. Hey, rookies ain't playing a ton. I'm playing some minutes, but then I'm not getting no quality minutes. And so me and Moses happened to live in the same building. Moses lived in the penthouse, I lived on like the sixth floor, if I remember correctly. And I said, "Mo, can I come see you tonight?" And he said, "Sure." And I call him "Dad" even to this day. And one of the most bitter-sweet things, his family knew how close we were. I got to do the eulogy at his funeral. I loved that dude. So I go up. I said, "Big Mo, why am I not getting no play?" He said, "Oh, young fella, you're fat and you're lazy."

Over his sixteen-year career, **CHARLES BARKLEY** won a league MVP in 1993 and was selected to eleven All-Star games and eleven All-NBA teams. Post-playing career, he's become a fixture in the media world, where he currently co-hosts *Inside the NBA*.

MATT BARNES: Plain and simple.

CHARLES BARKLEY: I'm like, "What?" He says, "You're fat and you're lazy." He said, "Charles, you can't play at 300 pounds in the NBA, young fella. You're too fat and too lazy. Can't work hard at 300 pounds." And I went downstairs and cried, not going to lie, but he said, "You want to lose weight? I'll come meet you before practice. I'll meet you after practice." And I said, "Please." And this dude says, "Let's . . ." And he did it in a way. That's how smart he was, he did it in a way. He says, "Let's lose 10 pounds." He met me before practice, met me after practice. I get to 290 and I notice, even that 10 pounds, I'm like, "I can work a little bit harder." He says, "Okay, let's lose 10 more." I'm like, "Okay." I get to 280. Now I'm actually getting to play. He says, "Let's lose 10 more." Now, I'm at 270. Now I'm really getting to play. There's numbers I can work. I mean, 30 pounds a lot. I get to 260. Now I'm starting. Now I'm really working my ass out. He says, "I want to try something." He says, "Let's get to 250." I'm like, "Okay, shit working, I'm good." I get to 250. Now, I'm really starting, things are really starting to take off. I actually got to 240, but I said, "But I don't feel strong." He said, "250 is your weight."

STEPHEN JACKSON: Wow.

CHARLES BARKLEY: But he was so smart. If he had told me to lose 50 pounds, I'd be like, "There's no fucking way I can lose 50 pounds. There's no way." And I lost the 50 pounds and the rest is history. But for that guy taking me under his wing, first of all, he was already one of the best to ever do it. For him to take a little fat kid under his wing, it changed my whole life. It changed my whole life. And that's why I called him "Dad."

ISAIAH THOMAS

MATT BARNES: What's the best piece of advice Nipsey ever gave you?

ISAIAH THOMAS: I think to never give up. Your race is your race. I remember one time he telling me, your race is your race. Don't ever compare it to nobody else's. I think throughout my whole career, I always took that and ran with it. Especially in our profession, it's hard to not compare yourself to the next dude. Especially when dudes is getting paid and you play the same position and you producing the same. Once he told me that back in, before I got to the league, I took that and ran with it. I was never worried about what the next man was doing. I was always worried about and focused on my marathon and my race. My shit is going to be different than anybody else's. How can I compare mine to somebody else when we're running two different marathons, two different races. I think that's probably the best advice he gave me, I take it in to this day.

QUINN COOK

I think the biggest thing that Coach K taught us when I was there and myself is the next play, next play in life, next play in basketball. Obviously in basketball, if you make a three, you can't fucking celebrate and pump your chest. You've got to get back on defense. You turn a ball over, you can't hold your head and keep that turnover in your head. But for me in life, it's like, Shit. You get cut from a team. Man, next opportunity, next phase in your life. If you don't get that job, if you fail that test, you can't dwell on your failures. You've got to let the failures keep pushing you to be great. Then the flip side is if you get to the league, you can't just spend your money and think you made it because for me, it was so hard getting in the league. It's even harder staying in the league. Obviously, you guys know that. Next plan in life is just keeping that mindset. Man, we've got to keep going, got to keep moving, got to work.

QUINN COOK is a two-time NBA champion who made his way to the league after a stint in the D-League, where he was named the 2017 D-League All-Star MVP. Cook also won an NCAA championship in 2015 with Duke.

MAGIC JOHNSON

MATT BARNES: Dr. J is someone you looked up to. I heard in college he rolled out the red carpet to you. Explain that story about Dr. J.

MAGIC JOHNSON: Yeah. So I was leaving school and I called him up. And so I said, "Hey, what is it like leaving? You left, so I want you to tell me what it's like for me to leave Michigan State early." And so he was explaining to me on the phone and then he said, "I'm going to do you one better. Fly out to Philly and hang out with me for the weekend." I said, "What? No, Doc."

MATT BARNES: That's the Doc.

MAGIC JOHNSON: This is Dr. J.

STEPHEN JACKSON: Right.

MAGIC JOHNSON: Saying a young fella can come hang with him and he puts me up in his crib at the big mansion?

MATT BARNES: How'd he pick you up?

MAGIC JOHNSON: A limo. Come on, man. And so I'm sitting there in the living room and he's talking to me and I'm just zoning out. I can't even believe it. I've always had Docs on, and now I'm with him. Oh, it was crazy, man. So we hung out the whole weekend. His wife took great care of me as well. We went to a couple playoff games because he was in the playoffs. He gave me some great advice. And then, here it is, seven months later I'm playing the brother in the NBA Finals.

CHRIS WEBBER

CHRIS WEBBER: This is a good story. And I'm in DC and just, it's terrible. It's a whole bunch of stories, in the paper things going on. It's Mike Tyson, dog, on everything I love. I have a security camera out there. And a friend of ours is bringing Mike to the crib. He's the champ. This is when he's suspended.

MATT BARNES: What year is this?

CHRIS WEBBER: '97. He's suspended, and I'm in DC. So in '97, I think, '98, and I'm in the crib and I'm going through it. And Tyson knocking on my door, ringing the bell. I don't answer. You know, I come out 20 minutes later, he knocking on the door. He then sits down on the porch. Then he started talking

CHRIS WEBBER played fifteen years in the NBA and is regarded as one of the most flashy and talented big men of all time. A five-time All-Star, 1994 Rookie of the Year, and Basketball Hall of Famer, Webber's career was loaded with accolades. However, the most iconic part of his basketball journey was his time spent with the University of Michigan's "Fab Five" team.

like, "I know you in there. I know you in there." You know what I'm saying? I'm try-ing to avoid it. You know what I mean? He my favorite fighter in the world. But what am I going to talk to you about right now? You don't even know me now. Right? Come in the basement, man. I keep a journal. And I just wrote down: one of the smartest men I've ever met, I needed this. And it was him like, "Man, I care about what people saying about you." He's like, "I run this hill every day." He's like, "The hill will never beat me in my life. The hill doesn't move, but it can't beat me. You know, the hill don't even want to attack me, but the hill will never beat me. Whatever I put in my mind, won't beat me. Won't beat me." Just like the hill can't beat you. And nothing you do here, you ain't even got to go to the hill. But in your mind, it'll beat you. And he was just talking about, man, just forgiving yourself, hard work, keeping that grind in you and understanding that. Like putting things in different places, but just not letting them overcome each other. And at the end of the day, I'm like, "Why'd you come over here?" What is it? He was like, "I just wanted to talk to you, brother." And he left, he's been my man a hundred grand ever since, but I never asked for that.

Fatherhood

10

pride in

being a father

JAYSON TATUM

Fatherhood is unlike anything I thought it was going to be. I found out I was going to have a kid at the end of the last month or two of college. I was nineteen at the time. I moved to Boston, moved my family out here. I got drafted. My world just got turned upside down, all in the span of six months. And I remember, I was so nervous, because I was so worried and concentrated. Like I'm going to be one of the best, I'm going to be a star. Like I'm not going to let nothing get in that way. Now I've got a son, and I want to be the best father I can be. I look at it as a challenge. I'm going to do both. I'm going to be one of the best in the league, and I'm going to be there with him every step of the way. And it's been a joy. I mean, I got help. His mom is up here. And my mom helps me out a lot, obviously, with traveling. Any chance I get, I'm always with him. I take more pride in being a father than I do being a basketball player.

LOU WILLIAMS

MATT BARNES: I had just signed, the year I won a championship with Golden State, 2017, I signed a three-year deal earlier with Sacramento. One night we were sitting up watching TV and they're just like, "Daddy, we miss when you used to take us to school."

LOU WILLIAMS: Yeah.

MATT BARNES: And that shit broke my whole heart.

LOU WILLIAMS: So my daughter did that to me one time. Last year, I was packing my bag and she was laying on my bed on her iPad. She said, "Daddy, can I ask you a question?" I said, "What's up?" She said, "You don't get tired of leaving us?"

MATT BARNES: Mm-hmm.

STEPHEN JACKSON: Damn.

LOU WILLIAMS: I was on my way out the door for a road trip and that shit broke my heart.

DWYANE WADE

DWYANE WADE: You know it's tough being a weekend parent first of all.

MATT BARNES: Yep.

DWYANE WADE: When you get your kids on the weekend, they want to have fun. You got to be the fun parent.

MATT BARNES: Right.

DWYANE WADE: But you're also trying to parent them.

MATT BARNES: Mm-hmm.

DWYANE WADE: That's one of the toughest things to do. It's an easier job when it comes to the responsibilities.

MATT BARNES: Mm-hmm.

STEPHEN JACKSON: Mm-hmm.

DWYANE WADE: You know what I'm saying? And it was the simple stuff. Like they were here for the weekend, now they're staying, so now I'm like, Oh, okay. What kind of beds they need?

MATT BARNES: Yeah.

DWYANE WADE: What kind of sheets they need?

MATT BARNES: Their school clothes.

DWYANE WADE: Like I got to think of everything.

MATT BARNES: Everything.

DWYANE WADE: Their this, their that, all the stuff I need to teach them now. So at first it was like I won custody, and I had an emotional moment. Then it snapped back into me that I had so much to teach them, and I had so much responsibility coming my way. I had to put so many people around them. You know that I need to find people to trust to put around my kids. Because of my job, and my career, it takes me away from being around. So it's definitely tough, it's not easy at all. Being a single parent is not an easy thing, but ultimately you're going to do what's best for your kids. Like I told my boys, we learn on the fly, we learn together.

KOBE BRYANT

I mean, we just try to raise our girls to be strong, independent women, you know what I'm saying? Hold themselves to really high standards.

BRADLEY BEAL

BRADLEY BEAL: Honestly, I think, I feel like there's nothing like fatherhood. And I feel like you have to be a father to really understand that. And coming up on two years, my oldest son . . . I have two boys. Bradley the second and Braylon. And so Bradley is coming up on two. But when he was born, I feel like it changed my life in so many ways for the better. But it gave me this motivation to where I was living for something bigger than myself.

MATT BARNES: That's true.

I can drop the ball today and take care of my kids for the rest of my life and be cool. —BRADLEY BEAL

BRADLEY BEAL: Everything that I was doing in life, it was bigger than me. Whether it was business, my mentality, my character, how I carry myself, my work ethic, how I hooped. It was like, every time I stepped on the floor, I'm like, Shit. These kids grow up in the day of YouTube and Instagram and Twitter. Like every game that you play is going to be on TV. So how do you carry yourself? How you interact with your teammates, like how you interact with fans, like all of that's going to be visible. So how do you want to portray [yourself] to your son?

MATT BARNES: Grateful.

BRADLEY BEAL: How do you treat wifey? Like all of that shit matters. So when he was born it was like . . . Man, it was an eye-opener for me. And honestly, man, I feel like it's nothing like it. Like I can drop the ball today and take care of my kids for the rest of my life and be cool.

ERNIE JOHNSON

MATT BARNES: You're a father of six, two biological, four adopted. I find that very interesting because that's what my mom wanted to do was adopt, but unfortunately she passed from cancer in '07. So talk to us just about fatherhood, everything you fought through in your personal health life to still be here and be the father you are for your children.

Sportscasting legend **ERNIE JOHNSON JR.** has been on the big screen for over forty years. He currently hosts the award-winning show *Inside the NBA*.

ERNIE JOHNSON: Cheryl Ann and I are blessed. You get married in '82, you get a boy in '84, you get a girl in '87, it's like, "Okay."

MATT BARNES: We're good.

ERNIE JOHNSON: We're set. That's good. Let's not mess with that. And then the unscripted part of your life kicks in because my wife has this wonderful heart.

STEPHEN JACKSON: We know because you talk about her so highly on the show. We all feel like we know your wife, man.

ERNIE JOHNSON: I know. Well, I apologize for doing that, I just can't stop it.

STEPHEN JACKSON: No, don't apologize man.

ERNIE JOHNSON: I come home from work one day and she says, "You know what we need to do?" And I'm like, "Chicken or fish, whatever you feel like. I'll eat anything." And she's like, "We need to go to Romania and get one of these kids out of an orphanage over there." Because she had seen the ABC News *20/20* about these kids just warehoused in this thing. And they're special-needs kids, they were being forgotten. She goes. I stay here. I'm in Atlanta with our kids, who are like three and seven at the time.

MATT BARNES: Oh, they were still babies.

ERNIE JOHNSON: Yeah. So I'm taking care of them. She's more worried about them than she is about her trip to Romania. She's like, "Man, I'm going to come home and those kids are not going to have had a vegetable for three months."

STEPHEN JACKSON: Mother's love.

ERNIE JOHNSON: We had a lot of pizza and Putt-Putt while she's over there. But she goes over there and finds this little boy who has got all these issues and calls me from Romania and says, "This boy is so much more than we can handle. He's three years old, he can't walk, he can't talk." And she says, "But I just can't imagine going the rest of my life wondering what happened to this kid." I was like, "Bring him home." And he had issues, still does. And then he gets diagnosed with muscular dystrophy and there's no cure for that. And a lot of the times, kids don't get out of their teens. Guy's thirty-two now, man. I've got this thirty-two-year-old miracle at my house. And he's on a ventilator. Can't do anything on his own. But he's amazing.

STEPHEN JACKSON: You guys are so amazing for that.

KENYON MARTIN

So, my favorite thing about fatherhood is just watching him grow, man, and being able to put what I didn't have into them. What I would've wanted in a father . . . To be there. To always be present, to be there, you know what I'm saying? To be able to laugh and joke and knowing somebody got my back no matter what.

> My favorite thing about fatherhood is just watching him grow, man, and being able to put what I didn't have into them. —KENYON MARTIN

CC SABATHIA

I lost my dad in 2013, we were real close. I was twenty-three years old. The same year, my son was born. It's been fun to kind of grow up and kind of turn into my dad. A lot of the shit I say to my son, I be like, "Damn, I'm my dad." It's fun to be a dad, man. It makes sports easy. You know what I'm saying? I come home after a game, they don't care if I threw a no-hitter or gave up seven runs. It's like, "Dad's home, time to play, fuck everything else." That kind of, because I'm super-intense when it comes to sports, so that kind of took my edge off a little bit. It helped me out a lot.

CARSTEN CHARLES "CC" SABATHIA JR. is a World Series champion pitcher, six-time MLB All-Star, Cy Young Award winner, and one of nineteen pitchers to amass over three thousand strikeouts.

ICE CUBE

Being able to teach, being able to teach them the game and the pitfalls that's out there for them. Being able to put them up on the intricate workings of this world, putting them up on that game as much as possible. So just being able to get him stability, making sure they are not some of those same old statistics because of my actions, you know what I'm saying? So it's just been great to see them become respectable grown men. They're just good people. And to me, that's the biggest accomplishment, is that they're good people.

> And to me, that's the biggest accomplishment,
> is that [my kids are] good people. —ICE CUBE

Their mothers be hot when they come out looking just like you. —THE GAME

RYAN LEAF

Best thing I've ever done. There's something about when they lay him in your arms and you realize, or this wave of selflessness just overwhelms you. Like everything I do from this point on is going to be about him. That's it. And I'm fearful. DNA, mental illness, I'm fearful of all those things, but I also have a lot more knowledge on how to go about being a dad differently. My dad, I love him. He's my hero. He came home from the war, they spit on him. He wasn't really vulnerable or transparent or anything like that. So I never saw it. I want my son to

RYAN LEAF is a former NFL quarterback and mental health activist. He was the second-overall pick in the 1998 NFL Draft.

understand fully that it's okay to show your emotions. That it's not weakness, it's actually a strength, and you'll be more relatable to people and everything like that. So, I mean, he's only four right now. All he cares about is gymnastics training. He calls it ninja training right now. He cares about that. Transformers and his swords. And so we're working on the things that we need to work on. I got a great partner who helps me along the way. And she knows me better than anybody so she can call me on my shit better than anybody.

JR SMITH

MATT BARNES: What's the best part about being a dad to you? Best part?

JR SMITH: Every time I walk in the house, it's Christmas.

T.I.

MATT BARNES: Fatherhood. Your kids are taking their journey, and you and your wife are working hard so you can provide a better upbringing for them. Explain your journey with each of them because it's been well documented. I remember the one time, did you do it on social media where you caught King smoking a joint in the spa the first time?

T.I.: We was on vacation, right? And so what I was talking about during that live was, "These rich kids, all they do is live off the fat of the land. They ain't got to work for nothing." And he happened to have been with his shirt off like Scarface in the Jacuzzi.

MATT BARNES: Right. It was perfect timing, right.

T.I.: Kicked back, like he paid for everything.

MATT BARNES: It's his house.

T.I.: I went to show him being in the Jacuzzi and this nigga's smoking a joint.

STEPHEN JACKSON: It's lit!

T.I.: And I guess the cat was released out that bag that day and that was the first time I had ever seen him smoking.

MATT BARNES: Fatherhood on the fly.

JR SMITH played sixteen years in the NBA and is a two-time NBA champion. In high school he was named co-MVP of the 2004 McDonald's All-American game. Smith also earned the 2013 NBA Sixth Man of the Year award as a member of the New York Knicks, averaging a career-high 18.1 points off the bench.

PAUL GEORGE

So I'm a girl dad full-on. It's dope to see yourself in a little girl version. It's just a different world, it's a different joy, a different excitement to be able to be in a fatherhood.

WILL SMITH

Oh, man, fatherhood. If I had to say something to guide someone about it, first and foremost, everybody sucks at the beginning. It's okay. It's okay to not be good at it. It's okay to make mistakes. And the best thing you can do for your kids is learn and grow yourself. When we're trying to force our kids to do stuff and understand things that we didn't do that we didn't understand, they see the bullshit.

WILL SMITH went from rapper to one of the most famous actors in Hollywood in what seemed like the blink of an eye. This interview with Smith was one of his first public appearances following his altercation with Chris Rock at the 2022 Academy Awards.

> Oh, man, fatherhood. If I had to say something to guide someone about it, first and foremost, everybody sucks at the beginning. It's okay. It's okay to not be good at it. It's okay to make mistakes. —WILL SMITH

CARON BUTLER

STEPHEN JACKSON: Father of five, what does that mean to you?

CARON BUTLER: Everything. Because growing up without a father, obviously it left a huge stain on a lot of things. But it also taught me about having that void and what I wanted to be if I became a father. So it means everything.

At thirteen years old, **CARON BUTLER** was already a father with a long criminal record. Born and raised in Racine, Wisconsin, the odds were stacked against him from the jump. Despite being dealt a tough hand, Butler transformed his life in his teenage years. The result? A fourteen-year NBA career with two All-Star selections and a 2011 championship. He's currently an assistant coach for the Miami Heat.

DeSEAN JACKSON

Fatherhood, man. It's huge to me. I look at fatherhood as: What do I want my kids to hear about me when they grow up, and they become older? What are people going to say about their dads?

DeSEAN JACKSON is one of the most explosive wide receivers in NFL history. He's the all-time leader in touchdowns of sixty-plus yards with twenty-six.

KOBE BRYANT

KOBE BRYANT: When I took Gianna to the Laker game, that's the first Laker game I had been to I think since my jersey retirement.

STEPHEN JACKSON: Really?

KOBE BRYANT: We just had so much fun. Because for the first time, I was seeing the game through her eyes. It wasn't me sitting there as an athlete or a player or something like that. It was her. Like, she was having such a good time and the players were coming up and saying hi to her. 'Bron was talking about her fadeaway and all. It was exciting, and she had such a great time. As a father—

MATT BARNES: That's all you want. That's all you can ask for.

KOBE BRYANT: Yes, man. Yes, yes.

STEPHEN JACKSON: We both have girls. When it's time for that first date, are they going to get that Mamba, 81 points stare? You going to give the boy the stare like, "Look, bro, I put 81 on the court, don't make me put 81 of these on you."

KOBE BRYANT: I think it's implied.

MATT BARNES: He already knows.

We just had so much fun. Because for the first time, I was seeing the game through her eyes. —KOBE BRYANT

Mental Health

11

figure out a way

That's the last thing you should do, is keep it bottled up. —LIL WAYNE

to get it out

LIL WAYNE

STEPHEN JACKSON: You spoke recently on mental health, your struggles with it, and how it impacted you at a young age. What would be your message to anyone that is struggling with mental illness right now and kind of keeping it bottled up?

LIL WAYNE: That's the last thing you should do is keep it bottled up. And these days are different, man, you got so many outlets. Back then we couldn't just find an app or somebody to talk to. We couldn't do that. It was different.

MATT BARNES: Back then, we really couldn't even speak on it.

LIL WAYNE: Speak on it, yeah.

MATT BARNES: It was just you crazy.

LIL WAYNE: With that said, if you are going through any type of mental stress, the last thing to do is keep it to yourself. That doesn't mean go speak to someone else. If you can't accomplish that, sometimes you literally can't do that. Try your hardest. You got to figure out a way to get it out. For me, it was the pen and pad.

BONZI WELLS

BONZI WELLS: I remember when I was thirty-two years old and knowing I still got a little bit of action still in me. But I couldn't get a job. I end up fucking going to China. No disrespect to China, but it's like '09. I'm one of the first real tenured NBA players that went to China, and it's serious over there. But I'm over here shitty, I'm averaging like 40. I'm shitty because . . . I'm a league dude.

MATT BARNES: Right.

LIL WAYNE is regarded as one of the most influential hip-hop artists of all time and one of the best lyricists ever. Wayne's catalogue is filled with smash hits, and his trophy cabinet is highlighted by five Grammy Awards.

GAWEN DEANGELO "BONZI" WELLS played ten years in the NBA and was a mainstay on the Portland Trail Blazers in the early 2000s. He holds the Ball State men's basketball record for most points scored (2,485) and steals (347), and his number 42 jersey was retired by the university. He started his head coaching career at LeMoyne-Owen College in 2021 before joining Damon Stoudamire's coaching staff at Georgia Tech in 2023.

BONZI WELLS: And that was tough for me. So between 2009 and 2014, I don't even really remember that shit because I was going through so much mentally. I remember around that time I was just partying. I was out the league. I was partying. I was gambling every day. I was chasing, you know what I'm saying? And I ended up losing my woman, my kids, all that shit goes when you out the league and all that shit. So I was just going through all that bullshit. And I remember just having a dark day and I probably needed to talk to somebody. But we're too prideful to talk to people, and I just remembered and I just really appreciated . . . I'd hug him every time I see him. It was like 2014 and I'm sitting back and I was having a pity party for myself and I ended up watching Iverson, who had a documentary and he was talking about what he was going through in 2009 when the phone stopped ringing, he was going through all this shit. And I just remember I just started crying like a motherfucker. And I was like, Damn, it wasn't just me. And I didn't have his number but I wanted to reach out to him. And it kind of helped me snap out of it and kind of just get on with my life, you know what I'm saying? And that just helped me tremendously, which I probably needed to talk to somebody but I just appreciate that documentary when I watched it and I just saw like, Shit, I'm having a pity party like it's just me.

MATT BARNES: Right.

BONZI WELLS: But I wasn't thankful for all the stuff God had already given me. You know what I'm saying? I'm over here worried about the stuff that, you know, what I was . . . I'm from the hood, I ain't never had nothing. My family's huge. I was able to put my brothers and sisters through college, buy my parents' homes. Do all the shit we do. So I didn't think about those blessings, I was worried about the other shit. So I kind of snapped out of it and started moving on my life.

So between 2009 and 2014, I don't even really remember that shit because I was going through so much mentally. —BONZI WELLS

JAYLEN BROWN

MATT BARNES: Talk to us about that anxiety, because that's something when we first came in the league, mental health wasn't discussed, and you've been vocal with it. Kevin Love's been vocal with it. Other guys have been vocal with it. Putting that out, did you feel like that took a weight off your shoulders, or explain that to me.

JAYLEN BROWN: It didn't take a weight off my shoulders because I know that people still battle. It's a battle that still currently is.

MATT BARNES: Daily, right?

JAYLEN BROWN is a star forward currently playing for the Boston Celtics. He's made three All-Star teams and is currently the vice president of the NBA Players Association.

JAYLEN BROWN: It's going on, it's daily, everybody deals with it in some way, shape, or form. That voice is telling you, as good as you think you are, or what you're trying to do, or you're not worthy. Our kids, the younger generation, they deal with that on a daily basis. Me, I'm just using it as somebody of influence that goes through it, just so maybe they can feel a little bit more comfortable for it. But, for me, I don't say this like I overcame it or it's gone. It's just a daily battle. It was tough because when you get put into a situation with adversity, naturally you start to question yourself and your ability.

MATT BARNES: That's the first thing you do.

JAYLEN BROWN: And your confidence, like am I as good as I thought I was? As soon as you start to question yourself, it's over. As soon as you start to not believe in yourself, you can kiss it goodbye. As soon as they get in your head, the self-doubt is going to kill you before anybody else can even touch you. So, for me, that's why I had a rough start to last year, because it took me a minute to get out of that, to like, okay, remind myself of what I bring to the table, remind myself of who I am, remind myself that I'm unique.

MATT BARNES: Jaylen Brown, Goddammit.

JAYLEN BROWN: And I'm okay with that.

CARI CHAMPION

CARI CHAMPION: For me, I've always felt bad for the athletes. I have had empathy and now that I can see and be able to help and witness that a lot of these young boys, even grown men, are coming out saying, "I need help. I'm struggling. Life is hard. I'm not as tough as I'm trying to make you all feel. I don't care how much money I got, how many chains I got, how many broads I got."

STEPHEN JACKSON: "I cry."

CARI CHAMPION: "I cry." Shit is hard. "I'm having a mental breakdown. Today is tough." We were able to do a story with one athlete and the fact that he said he was getting help

and starting to get help and feeling a little more easy, not thinking about taking his life. Those kinds of messages that I get are rewarding. That's what we're here to do. We're here to help and tell really great stories. Of course there's fun stuff, but to me that's huge because in our community, you know well, you're supposed to be taught to be strong, be strong, be strong. Be strong. But it's okay to say, "I'm not as strong." It's okay to say, "I hurt. Like my mind is not right."

STEPHEN JACKSON: They've been teaching us to be strong and to be able to take so much, but they don't teach being real with yourself enough. You know what I mean? And that's when you start to turn the corner when you're being real with yourself. Yeah, you can be tough as hell, but you got to be real with yourself when you're dealing with life and everything you're going through. You know what I mean? Don't live by a façade, be real with yourself and that'll make it a lot easier.

CARI CHAMPION: It's hard for everybody to be real. It's hard. Because you don't want people to see. Men are in general, in my opinion, hard. They're not expressive. Very few men like to talk about their feelings. You want to go in a cave and figure it out. So then you want me to turn around and tell you that I feel weak and I haven't figured it out and I'm vulnerable, and all these emotions that you're just not familiar with that make you feel like somebody could take advantage of you in a world where people do nothing but take advantage of you.

DeMAR DeROZAN

DeMAR DeROZAN: It's crazy because I find myself having a conversation with people that people would never think has something going on. To be able to have that dialogue with people, and you see the weight lift off their shoulders from just feeling comfortable with another person that knows they've been through something. You feel different.

MATT BARNES: That's dope. We definitely commend you for your bravery because, like you said, it's tough. A lot of people don't have the courage to speak up on it, and you put it out there. You're able to use it as a vehicle to help others, which is dope, man. Good work with that.

DeMARCUS COUSINS

MATT BARNES: What's the toughest part about this rehab process and not being able to do what you love?

DeMARCUS COUSINS: The toughest part is missing basketball. I love to hoop. I'm not the tall guy that just hoop because—

STEPHEN JACKSON: I'm tall.

MATT BARNES: You got some game.

DeMARCUS COUSINS: A little bit. So you know what I'm saying. I really love this game and being away from that alone is hard enough, not even including everything else that comes with being away from it, so.

STEPHEN JACKSON: That's what gets lost in translation, though, especially with athletes. When we go through ups and downs, even with me with the brawl shit, when I got suspended thirty games. I was away from the game, that was probably one of the lowest points in my life because I played basketball my whole life. Nobody could take basketball from me. I can go play it on the park, I go play it everywhere. So when the game was taken from me—what I've been doing my whole life—that shit took me down more than anything somebody can say about me, more than anything somebody could do about me, because that's what I love most. So when you go through stuff, people want to look at that, but don't look at . . . They don't understand that you just love the fucking game. You just want to play the game.

DeMARCUS COUSINS: Absolutely, at the end of the day, that's what we all—

MATT BARNES: That's why we do it.

DeMARCUS COUSINS: Well, most of us.

STEPHEN JACKSON: Right.

DeMARCUS COUSINS: That's what we love to do. So just being away from that part, that shit sucks. But you deal with everything else that comes with it.

STEVE NASH

MATT BARNES: Thirty-eight, coming to LA to play with Kobe, Lakers signed Dwight [Howard]. Talk to us about that time.

STEVE NASH: Yeah, it was exciting. I mean, the big, my first priority was I was going through a divorce. I wanted to come to LA over Toronto and New York, the other two options, because it was close to Phoenix, and it was so much uncertainty going through that period. So that was the number one reason. But then, to be able to join forces with those players, obviously thought we had a championship opportunity, and couldn't

have been more wrong or gone more sideways, but coming here I was excited. I actually, I think, made my last All-Star Game that season at thirty-eight before I came to the Lakers. So I still believed I could have a big impact. And I don't know how much of it was I was losing a step or how much of it was me breaking my knee at the start of that season, breaking my tib-fib joint. I know I was never the same after I fractured my knee, but the whole thing, Dwight was coming off back surgery.

MATT BARNES: I think he rushed back.

STEVE NASH: Yeah.

MATT BARNES: I think he rushed back, because I had Dwight in Orlando, and when I tell you, I've never played with a more security blanket in my life, he was incredible. And it hurt me because I knew, when you come to Lakers, you can contest to it, it's just a different aura. You're expected to win. You're expected to be your best. There's no excuses. Fuck everything else. You're a Laker. So nothing else matters.

STEVE NASH: Right, sure.

MATT BARNES: So him coming back, rushing back, I personally knew that he wasn't ready. But I think you alluded to something, too, that people don't think about. The process is in the mental preparation, the mental toughness, you're going through a divorce, you know what I mean? So you're still trying to put yourself in a position of uncertainty . . . I still want to be able to see my kids, I don't want to move too far away.

Without getting too far into your personal life, talk to us about that, because people don't see that side of athletes and realize how important other stuff in our life is when it pertains to our craft and our profession.

STEVE NASH: Yeah, I think anyone could, if you took a second to examine that, how difficult that would be. I would fly back sometimes after practice to go to my, well, how old would the girls have been? They must've been eight, nine years old. Go back for a soccer practice and fly back after it. I just—

MATT BARNES: Right. Just to see them.

STEVE NASH: Just to see them, to get those touches in, so to speak. And get through that school year. They moved to LA after the school year. But, yeah, I mean it adds to it, right? It adds to everything. And maybe at that stage of my career, the stress didn't help when I'm trying to overcome so many things. But it just wasn't meant to be. And I've never worked as hard in my life as I did for those two years, trying to make it happen, trying to contribute, trying to be near my best or at a level that could really contribute, and it was an exciting prospect, and at the end it was a disaster. But still a great experience. So many times when you go through difficult times, it's tough in the moment, but when you get through the other side, you realize that you learn a lot. You were challenged. You're growing.

MATT BARNES: Oh, man. So much.

TRACY McGRADY

TRACY McGRADY: Yeah. I was depressed, bro. I've never been depressed in my life. I was depressed, man. I was in Chicago doing my rehab and I had to lay in my bed for eight hours with my leg in a machine for eight weeks. You talk about depression. And then I'm watching my boys on TV compete without me. I'm here in Chicago. I was messed up, never been in that situation. The great thing about it, my kids, once the summer came, 'cause this happened in February when I had my surgery and then once my kids got out of school they all, my family, came to Chicago and that really helped me get through it. But I was up there by myself and it was, well, I was out of there, bro. I was like, Man, fuck this game. I don't even want to play no more. Mentally, I was ejected from the game.

MATT BARNES: Well, it seems like you got to think like me. You have the world screaming your name, one second cheering for you T-Mac this, T-Mac that. I got my own shoe. I missed some that . . . And then—

TRACY McGRADY: Gone!

MATT BARNES: —you're all by yourself in a dark room in Chicago with nobody to turn to.

TRACY McGRADY: Gone, gone. You went from MVP chants with 20,000 people, entertaining at the highest level. And I can't even reach that level no more. I don't get no chance. It went from T-Mac to Tracy. Hey, what up, Tracy? Oh, what up dog . . . It ain't T-Mac no more. He's gone.

Yeah. I was depressed, bro . . . I was like, Man, fuck this game. I don't even want to play no more. —TRACY McGRADY

JJ REDICK

MATT BARNES: I tell people, as athletes, we've been trained our whole life to give it all physically. Obviously, some mental comes with that, but I think my transition to my post-career, having an opportunity to work with ESPN, having an opportunity to work with Showtime and iHeart, this mental exhaustion is a fucking monster. I'm finished, after I have to host a few podcasts, or I have to do a bunch of stuff on ESPN. And it's a whole different kind of tired. Then, on top of that, I still got to chase my kids around. You have to do the same thing. But it's different. And I have a whole new respect for this life, because I got to do it at the highest level and physically exhaust everything I had in my body as a professional

The 2006 National College Player of the Year, **JJ REDICK** has been showcasing his unlimited range since his early days hooping in high school. He holds the record for most points and three-point field goals at Duke and his number 4 jersey is retired. Redick had a successful fifteen-year NBA career and transitioned into the media, where he hosts *The Old Man and The Three* podcast and is a featured analyst on ESPN.

athlete. And now, transitioning into this media space, this mental wear down and mental exhaustion is just different. It'll literally put you to sleep. I'm done.

JJ REDICK: I'm with you. There's some days where I'm gasping for air. I'm trying to come up out of the dirt, just to get a breath. Some of that, too, I mean, if you're a parent, and you're an active, involved, day-to-day parent . . . I'm with my kids and we're doing stuff. I'm taking them to school. I'm picking them up from school. And you're managing that, and then, for me, as a still-active player, you're managing that part of playing. Also, there's this mental fuckery that happens every day where you're like, All right. I didn't anticipate having to answer twenty emails every single day, nonstop, for the past two months. I didn't anticipate that. Three, four conference calls a week, I didn't anticipate that. I thought [it would be], "All right, just give me the guest. I'll do the interview." So that part of it, actually, as exhausting as it's been, has been super-fun, you do feel like—

MATT BARNES: Because you enjoy it. You still enjoy it. And you're learning.

JJ REDICK: You're owning it, and you're building it. It's a total learning process, totally. I've never done some of this stuff before, so it's been really awesome.

> There's some days where I'm gasping for air. I'm trying to come up out of the dirt, just to get a breath. **—JJ REDICK**

MAHMOUD ABDUL-RAUF

Whatever you focus on grows. So if you keep focusing on the negative, it's going to continue to be negative and it's going to show. They say your thinking influences your behavior. Your behavior forms your character, and your character determines your fate. So if you constantly thinking negative, negative, I can't do this and that, well, you going to end up in a bad position. So it goes either way.

MAHMOUD ABDUL-RAUF was blackballed from the NBA after he refused to stand during the National Anthem before games. When he was on the court, he shined, setting the LSU freshman scoring record with fifty-five points and winning Most Improved Player of the Year in 1993 with the Denver Nuggets.

TRAVIS KELCE

We reached a mountain peak and got crowned king, and you can't say anything about it. You know what, sometimes you just have to block it out and just tell them, "Fuck them." That's the mentality that you have to have. I used to, at a younger age in my career, really care about all of that to a certain extent, and it used to get to me. It used to get to me a lot, and I would get frustrated out on the field, not having the success that I thought I should have. You know what, I wasn't living a fun life, and mentally you have to be able to find happiness in what you're doing and block out a lot of the negativity that's going on. Mental health is such a huge part of being an athlete.

Three-time Super Bowl champion **TRAVIS KELCE** is regarded as one of the best tight ends ever to play in the NFL. He is a nine-time Pro Bowler and four-time First-Team All-Pro. He holds several records, including most postseason receptions (156), most seasons with 1,000-plus receiving yards at the tight end position (seven), and the most games with one hundred-plus receiving yards in the playoffs (eight). In addition to his legendary playing career, Kelce hosts the *New Heights* podcast with his brother, Jason, who is also a Super Bowl champion and considered one of the best centers in the league.

> You have to be able to find happiness in what you're doing and block out a lot of the negativity that's going on. Mental health is such a huge part of being an athlete. **—TRAVIS KELCE**

LAMAR ODOM

MATT BARNES: You touched on mental health and how that's never been something that we as Black men have discussed. It's a sign of weakness.

LAMAR ODOM: We always think it's cool for our dude to be a little crazy.

MATT BARNES: Yeah. Or just tough it out.

LAMAR ODOM: You know what I'm saying? And he might need help. But it's very important that we do get help. We can't be helping him lock us up.

Hailing from Queens, New York, **LAMAR ODOM** brought his city flair all the way to the NBA, where he played fourteen years and won two championships with the Lakers. At six-ten, Odom is one of the most fluid and skilled forwards that has ever played the game.

CHRIS BOSH

MATT BARNES: What was that transition like just to go and . . . now you're in the house every day with your family, and it's just you're watching your friends continue to move forward. Was there a mental block there or a mental frustration? Or anything you went through having to watch that?

CHRIS BOSH: So I knew I wasn't going to play after that. And then D got traded back to Miami later that year. And I was so happy for him but I was so hurt at the same time. Just him being able to get that chance to go back and have those moments. I felt I deserved them but I wasn't getting them. And it is what it is. A very small percentage of guys in the league get that. You realize how special that is. And then really I got to give credit to my family, man. They helped me together. We had just had our twins. They were super-young. They needed me, my wife needed me to kind of focus on the family. I had a lot of things I had to clean up from things in the past. So you don't know that but when you're done playing, you guys know, you got a lot of stuff.

MATT BARNES: A lot of free time.

CHRIS BOSH: A lot of free time too.

MATT BARNES: You don't realize how much—

STEPHEN JACKSON: A lot of cleaning up to do.

CHRIS BOSH: For sure.

MATT BARNES: You don't realize how much time basketball takes until you're not doing it no more.

CHRIS BOSH: For sure.

MATT BARNES: From even in the summertime when we're working out two or three times a day. And we're such creatures of habit, we don't realize what void that filled when we remove ourselves. I mean, if you think about it, we play our seasons eight or nine months if you're lucky. If you're lucky, then you take three or four months off, then you start training. So we're really on eleven out twelve months a year, we're on.

CHRIS BOSH: Yeah, for sure.

MATT BARNES: And then all of a sudden it's just not there no more. It's just like, Holy shit. I got a whole life to live. And, like you said, early thirties. You got a whole life in front of you still.

CHRIS BOSH: Oh, yeah. And my babies were babies. I had babies, we had babies. And that was a challenge. And especially for me, I realized how much my wife did. I remember one morning coming downstairs and all the kids were playing and I'm just like, "Damn, they're loud. They're so loud." I looked at my wife, "Are they always this loud?" She's like . . . you know?

MATT BARNES: Like every day, dude. What you talking about?

CHRIS BOSH: Yeah. I'm usually taking my pregame nap and she gets them into the play room so they could make noise there. And those things took some getting used to. But I like to say, hopefully I fell into the role of dad pretty good now and I've got a pretty good sense for what I'm doing. But at first it was a challenge kind of readjusting everything. And at the same time trying to figure out what the hell I'm going to do with the rest of my life and what kind of message I'm going to leave and all that stuff. I mean, I never saw myself not playing basketball at thirty-two. I wanted to play at least until thirty-six. I just turned thirty-six. So it's like, Damn. All right. Well, I'm in this position. I just have to learn how to be a civilian and figure this thing out.

BRANDON MARSHALL is a six-time NFL Pro Bowl wide receiver who played thirteen years in the league. He holds the NFL record for the most receptions in a single game (twenty-one). Outside of his celebrated playing career, Marshall has made his way into the media scene, previously co-hosting *First Things First* on Fox Sports and *Inside the NFL* on Showtime. He was nominated for an Emmy in 2016 for Outstanding Sports Personality. He currently hosts the *I Am Athlete* podcast.

BRANDON MARSHALL

This life is hard, and if you don't have a game plan around how you're going to deal with stress, that stress can turn into a mental health challenge and mental health issue for you. It may not be bipolar. It may not be borderline, but if you don't correct these things, then it can definitely hit you and hit you in a major way.

ISAIAH THOMAS

MATT BARNES: You've gone into great detail about the physical pain, day-to-day and even playing. Talk to us about that mental. You said your mental is riding and where you are mentally, because I'm sure the mental was more up fucked-up than your actual pain was.

ISAIAH THOMAS: The pain was obviously there but the mental was, like, I couldn't hide that. I couldn't fake that. You got to get through that somehow. With everything happening back-to-back, my sister passing and me getting hurt, getting traded three or four times in that small span of time.

STEPHEN JACKSON: You started questioning yourself.

ISAIAH THOMAS: For the first time in my life.

STEPHEN JACKSON: That's a lot, man.

ISAIAH THOMAS: Damn, is it over? Do I got to do something else? It was a lot for me, the mental part cooked me. At the end of the day, I always was like, Hoop is what I love. Until I can't do it no more, I'm going to try. I always told people, I'm like the easy thing to do at the end of the day is the quit. Anybody can walk in and quit and be like, I'm going to throw the towel in. I'm tapping out. The hard thing to do is when some real adversity hits you, to be okay, how do I get through that wall? How do I get through that adversity? I just stayed down. I stayed solid. I had the right people around me. I remember D. Rose telling me. D. Rose is one of my close homies. He told me when he was going through his shit, he was like, "I was trying to fight against everybody. Once I let that fight go, my mental just eased up." I was able to get through it all. During that time with Cleveland and jumping the teams and chasing that max. Once I was done with that and I had no more fight to prove to people. My mental just slowed all the way down. And then, shit, I did the surgery. I had no pain, no more. I'm like my money's good. I'm straight. My kids is healthy. One thing that kept me going was my little boys was watching me every day.

STEPHEN JACKSON: That's big.

ISAIAH THOMAS: Even though they would make jokes about, ah, you're not in the league no more, you're not, you used to be. You miss everything now. You used to make every- thing in Boston. That's what kept me going. I knew if I did lay down and tap out at some point in their life, they're going to tap out when some shit get real.

STEPHEN JACKSON: That's why we commend you, bro. That's another reason why we want to have you on the show. We like giving our brothers out their flowers.

It's a lot of mental hurdles and obstacles that you got to run through in order for you to reach your highest peak as an individual. —**KEVIN DURANT**

MAHMOUD ABDUL-RAUF

STEPHEN JACKSON: Let me ask you this question and it's a little off. Mental health, so I always tell people this, and I want your opinion on it. The things that I've seen growing up as struggling and hard, as hard as it was to make it out, that will cause mental health. I can't see myself having mental health issues today with the blessings that God has given me to change my life and my family's life. Can you say that someone, once they reach success and millions of dollars that they can still deal with mental health after seeing the things that we come from?

MAHMOUD ABDUL-RAUF: Yeah, that's tough. I think mental illness, you have billionaires and you have millionaires committing suicide.

STEPHEN JACKSON: Right.

MAHMOUD ABDUL-RAUF: And it's all about, when it's all said and done, it's all about perception. You know? Have people that are poor that are more at peace than people who are wealthy.

STEPHEN JACKSON: Right.

MAHMOUD ABDUL-RAUF: And you have people that are poor that are not at peace, and you have wealthy people that are at peace. So I think it eventually boils down to a state of mind. Yeah, we had it tough, but still life is tough.

KEVIN DURANT

MATT BARNES: What does the advancement in mental health in this era that players are more susceptible to talking about it mean to you?

KEVIN DURANT: Feel like every player wants to give a deeper perspective on what they go through as just men in general, especially in this life with this profession. It's a lot of mental hurdles and obstacles that you got to run through in order for you to reach

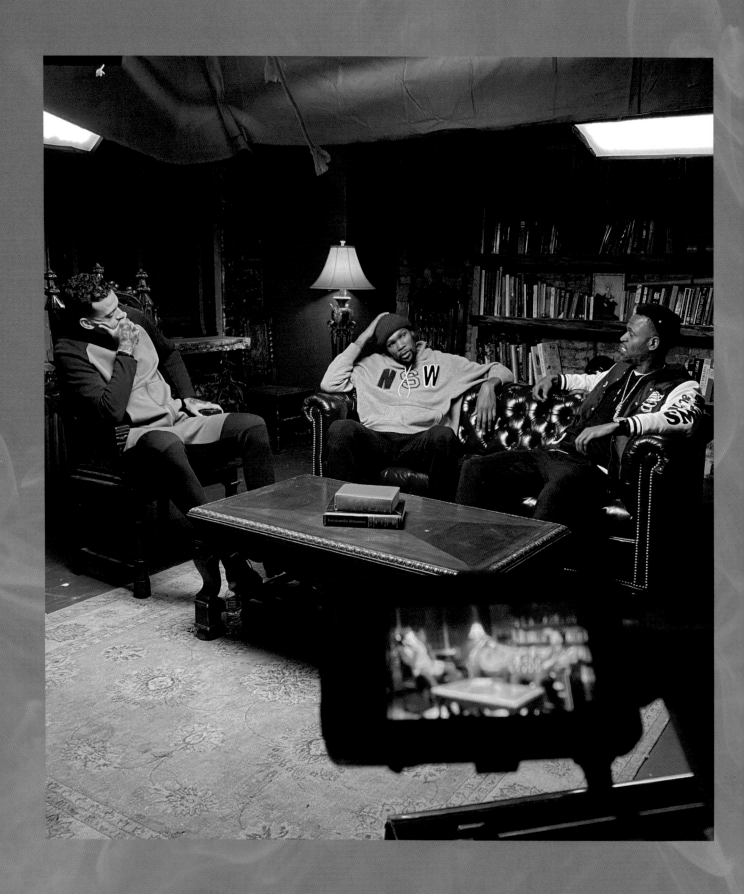

your highest peak as an individual. So whether it's the great times and/or whether it's the low points in your life, I feel like just having that perspective is only going to help others. And they had the courage to talk about it in front of people is something I enjoy seeing from my peers. There's no judgment from anybody, it's real open dope dialogue when it comes to it. I think it's a perfect time for it.

JERMAINE O'NEAL

JERMAINE O'NEAL: I remember my first six months of retirement, it was hell.

MATT BARNES: It's a lot.

JERMAINE O'NEAL: It was hell. I was, like, What am I supposed to do? I actually had shit going on but it was like, I remember sitting in my office and borderline felt depressed because I played in the NBA half my adult life. From seventeen to thirty-five.

MATT BARNES: You fill that void of competitive nature.

JERMAINE O'NEAL: You definitely missing something. The biggest thing that I missed was the fellas because we can go back into the communities and I have some great friends in Dallas, but it's different because they don't understand what we are. In many cases we're dealing with the same situation, whether it's family, relationships, whatever it may be. Some people can't digest that. They see, okay, you got money. You living in like this and what the fuck's wrong with you? Why are you mad? Why are you sad? They don't get that. I miss the bus rides, the locker rooms, the plane rides. I don't think nothing in life can ever replace that.

JERMAINE O'NEAL is known for being one of the most skilled NBA big men who jumped from high school straight to the professional ranks. He was a six-time NBA All-Star, made three All-NBA teams, and was the 2002 Most Improved Player of the Year. O'Neal was the linchpin for the Indiana Pacers in the early 2000s and helped lead his team to a league-best sixty-one wins in the 2003–04 season.

DAME DASH

DAME DASH: I get therapy every fucking week. It's like having a counselor.

MATT BARNES: Me too.

DAME DASH: You got to.

Depression sure knows how to kill a day. —LaRUSSELL

12
Hip-Hop

hearing hip-hop

and falling in love

RZA

RZA: Hip-hop was my first musical love, you know what I mean? Then the GZA, my older cousin, took me to a block party right in New York, Bronx, you know what I mean?

STEPHEN JACKSON: Mm-hmm, boogie down.

RZA: Yeah, Bronx, the birthplace of hip-hop, and I heard it. I heard, "Dip dip dive, so-socialize, clean out your ears and you open your eyes," you know what I did? I cleaned out my ears and I opened  my eyes, yo, and I live that and I'll never forget hearing hip-hop and falling in love with it, and knowing that that was my calling.

DJ QUIK

DJ QUIK: I just learned the five elements of hip-hop from Doug E. Fresh last week.

MATT BARNES: What's that?

DJ QUIK: DJing is number one. Two is the MC. Three is graffiti, four is breakdancing, and fifth is the human beatbox.

MATT BARNES: That's the five elements of hip-hop.

DJ QUIK: Yeah, I was like, "Word."

213

EBRO

Hip-hop's been a constant. I would say it's the most successful, longest-running, chart-dominating music genre.

THE GAME

STEPHEN JACKSON: If you could be remembered by one bar of lyric in your career, what would it be?

THE GAME: It would be . . . "I got shit on my chest, I must confess / Last night I was the nigga that shot up your projects / Now I'm back in the hood, with rocks in the Pyrex / Tan khakis and them Nike Airs with the dyed checks / I was forced to live this life, forced to bust my chrome / My pops left me in a foster home / I felt abandoned like Quik now that Mausberg gone / So I don't hop in the SS without the Mossberg homes."

COMMON

At a certain point, even just when I first started rhyming, I was like, Okay, I want to just be dope. I want niggas to know who I am. That's just the essence of why I love hip-hop. But then eventually, just looking around and seeing where I grew up, getting to go to different cities, I was like, Man, I got a chance to really be a voice for them, too, through the music.

FAT JOE

FAT JOE: I was just born in the South Bronx where hip-hop was created. So Melle Mel, I would watch Grandmaster Flash. My brother was a crate boy for Grandmaster Flash, Mr. Nas. So all these people were around my neighborhood for real. Lovebug Starski. And I would watch them play baseball.

MATT BARNES: How old were you seeing all this stuff?

FAT JOE: Kid. Seven years old, eight years old. I was blessed to grow up loving hip-hop just as a fan. And just to watch the evolution that hip-hop over the years is mind-blowing.

LUDACRIS

Atlanta is the Mecca, man. It's the Motown of the south, and people said that early on, but I'm sure after two decades of seeing what's going on in the industry and how prominent it is, there's no doubting that at this point.

LIL WAYNE

STEPHEN JACKSON: When people ask us what does basketball mean to us, my answer is kind of like everything because it changed my life. Got me out the hood. Is that the same kind of answer you would give if somebody asked you what hip-hop means to you?

LIL WAYNE: No.

MATT BARNES: What would your answer be?

LIL WAYNE: What hip-hop means to me . . . My answer would be everything. I look at hip-hop as what God created for me in my time. I believe that we all are just . . . Everything's happened before. And I mean not life, I'm just meaning in this world. The last generation, all the same shit happened. Generation before that.

STEPHEN JACKSON: They recycle.

LIL WAYNE: All the same shit. So back then, it was poets. You was holding people's attention and you was making the most of that attention. Which is figuring out how to put your thoughts to words, and figuring out how to make those words translate to the people that you're trying to talk to. Make it make sense

JOSEPH ANTONIO CARTAGENA, known to the world as **FAT JOE**, has been sharing his lyrical prowess since the early '90s. Born and raised in New York City, Fat Joe has delivered hit songs that have been played on radio airwaves for years, from 2003's "What's Luv?" to 2017's "All the Way Up." The founder of the Terror Squad, Fat Joe has collaborated with big-name artists and has been nominated for four Grammy Awards.

Rapper and actor **CHRISTOPHER BRIAN BRIDGES**, a.k.a. **LUDACRIS**, has helped bring eyes and ears to the Atlanta hip-hop scene since his debut single "What's Your Fantasy" in 2000. He followed that up with his album *Word of Mouf*, which was nominated for a Grammy Award for Best Rap Album in 2002. His fourth album, *Chicken-n-Beer*, debuted at number one on the US *Billboard* 200 and featured commercial hits "Stand Up" and "Splash Waterfalls," among others. Ludacris hit the acting scene with his role as Tej Parker in *2 Fast 2 Furious*, a role he has reprised six times since.

to them. So much sense that they not only like it, love it, they live by it. So I thank God that this is what my path was as one of those guys.

FAT JOE

STEPHEN JACKSON: How did the hip-hop in Miami grow when you arrived?

FAT JOE: Shit, we grew that motherfucker all the way. Miami's always been a place that embraced me, showed me love, made me happy. I come from the concrete jungle. New York City, no disrespect, but it's just a big, giant ghetto. Landing in the plane, you don't see no palm trees or no shit. You just see a big, metallic ghetto.

STEPHEN JACKSON: Bricks.

FAT JOE: So when I got to experience Miami and how the people are, how nice they were. I came up at a time where we were in each other's videos, everybody was celebrating each other. It had gotten into

a bad time where Dipset was arguing with Nas and I'm beefing with 50. New York rappers, it was just out of control. That's around the time I had met Cool & Dre, and I fell in love with them and Khaled. I said, "I'm moving to Miami." When I got there, I noticed that everybody wanted to work with each other. We had Lil Wayne in one studio, we had Ross in one studio, you had Pitbull in another studio, you had Khaled in the studio, you had me in the studio, and everybody's running in everybody's stuff, helping each other. I was like, Holy shit, this is what hip-hop's about, man. Everybody working with each other, helping each other out. We had lost that for a very long time in New York.

JADAKISS

STEPHEN JACKSON: Let me ask you this, though. How did the Allen Iverson commercial come about?

MATT BARNES: Oh, that shit was hard.

JADAKISS: See, that's another thing I don't get credit for. That's one of the first sports spots that went crazy.

JASON TERRANCE PHILLIPS, a.k.a. **JADAKISS,** is a New York rapper who, alongside friends and fellow artists Sheek Louch and Styles P, formed the trio The Lox. Later on, he embarked on a solo career in the early 2000s, releasing five solo studio albums.

STEPHEN JACKSON: That really connected rap and basketball.

JADAKISS: Connected hip-hop and basketball.

STEPHEN JACKSON: That connected it.

JADAKISS: They accepted it. Stern had to loosen up for that and be like, "Yo, this is good."

RICKY WILLIAMS

STEPHEN JACKSON: Your running style. What kind of music is that?

RICKY WILLIAMS: I came up in the nineties, so West Coast hip-hop. Right? It's smooth and then it hits you.

STEPHEN JACKSON: Yeah. Yeah.

MATT BARNES: Exactly. Smooth as a motherfucker and then it just hit.

WILL SMITH

MATT BARNES: When did music come into the picture for you?

WILL SMITH: Twelve years old, I started writing rhymes and that was just after "Rapper's Delight." When "Rapper's Delight" hit, it was over for me. It was like God telling me that's what I needed to do. And I heard that and I just knew. I don't know if it's the same thing with athletics, but you had that first time and you just know. It's like, I just love it. I love it. This is what I want to do. I found my power in words. I found just the essence of who I am in hip-hop.

I found just the essence of who I am in hip-hop.

—WILL SMITH

PENNY HARDAWAY

MATT BARNES: Hey, back when you were playing, who were you listening to to get ready for games?

PENNY HARDAWAY: I was listening to Jay, you know Jay and Biggie and Pac. That was them dudes back then.

STEPHEN JACKSON: Still are. They still are.

GILLIE AND WALLO

GILLIE: For us, it was like, I wrote my first rap in college playing around. Fucking around with some of my homies who had some equipment.

MATT BARNES: He didn't know?

GILLIE: And we just used to smoke some weed, rap some shit crazy, fall the fuck out laughing. And then one day they was like, "Let's write something to come back and record it." And it just so happened, when we came back, I was the first one to record and all them niggas were like, "Yo, nigga. What the fuck?" Literally, I'm like, "Nah, ain't no fucking rapper, man. Y'all niggas tripping, man." "Dog, that was hot." I'm like, "Yo, y'all tripping, man. Fuck is y'all talking about, man? I'm not no rapper." Then he heard the verse. "Yo, cuz." This thing was taking me everywhere. Talking about, "My cousin hot. He only got one rap."

MATT BARNES: He only got one rap.

STEPHEN JACKSON: I love that.

GILLIE: He only got one rap.

WALLO: That's all he needed.

KILLER MIKE

As a kid—hip-hop at nine years old, I got turned onto it. By the time I was twelve I turned out, it was what I was about. I was going to be a rapper. I was going to figure that out.

MICHAEL SANTIAGO RENDER, a.k.a. **KILLER MIKE**, was born and raised in Atlanta where he met Big Boi of Outkast and was featured on their Grammy-award winning song "The Whole World." Aside from Outkast, Killer Mike has also collaborated with Jay-Z, Twista, and other big name artists. Outside of music, Killer Mike is an activist and has also dabbled in acting.

So growing up, I'm sixteen in 1989, and hip-hop was at its peak. I remember me and J Rose used to write rhymes in class and pass them back to each other. Everybody who hooped wanted to be a rapper, and vice versa. **—CHRIS WEBBER**

ICE CUBE

STEPHEN JACKSON: Take us through the creation of *Straight Outta Compton.*

ICE CUBE: It was a fun record to make. You had Dre's undivided attention. To have Dr. Dre very hype and motivated is one of the best places artists can find themself in. In the room with Dre and he's hyped and motivated about making this song. What it's supposed to be. As long as you down to work, it's going to work. It ain't going to be just go in there and rap your lyrics and come out. He going to get every phrase and every line perfect. And so I knew, if I just went to the studio with some ideas. that he may pick a few of them, implement them into the song. And to see that process too is incredible. I think it was a lot of friendly competition because we was all trying to out-rhyme each other. D.O.C. doesn't get a lot of credit for writing a lot of those verses.

STEPHEN JACKSON: The D.O.C.

ICE CUBE: D.O.C. The D.O.C, too. he wrote a lot of that of Eazy's verses on not only his album but on N.W.A., too. So we was just all trying to outdo each other. Out-rhyme each other. And because Dre would tell you straight up, like if you ain't dope, you not going on the record.

SNOOP DOGG

MATT BARNES: Classic. That's the first song you and Dre did together?

SNOOP DOGG: That's the first song that we put out. We recorded "'G' Thang" before that. Yeah, but I had a motherfucking toothache and I went and got some pills from my auntie and violated my probation and had to go to jail for four months.

MATT BARNES: For real?

SNOOP DOGG: That prolonged that shit. Yep.

MATT BARNES: Y'all shot "'G' Thang" and then you got locked up?

SNOOP DOGG: We recorded "'G' Thang" first, then I got locked up, then I got out, and then we did "Deep Cover." "Deep Cover" came out first, and then we re-recorded "'G' Thang" once my shit got healed. My voice was fucked-up, but once my shit got healed, my shit was crisp as a mother-fucker. I heard that shit in my earphone. I'm like, "This nigga Dr. Dre is the shit." My shit sounded clean. One, two, three, and to the four. That shit was crystal clear. Because remember I was rapping on bullshit-ass equipment before I met this nigga. Imagine a nigga on a Walkman, then all of a sudden they get some Beats by Dre. To hear your voice like that, it's like, oh, man, this shit is mind-blowing.

13

Flowers

that shit's

I just want to say I'm proud of you guys man. I'm proud of you for your success.
—CHARLES BARKLEY

hard to do

CARI CHAMPION

First off, I have to say I'm so happy to be here because I work with you guys both and I don't know if people know this. Because they sit here and they see you guys and they're like, "Oh, they just talk and they have such fun and they are cool and they know people in the league." But you guys have really transitioned. That shit's hard to do. As an athlete to become a broadcaster you have a voice that people respect. Obviously, they respect you, but you do it so effortlessly. Both y'all. I think that nobody acknowledges that. The shit's not easy.

CHARLES BARKLEY

I just want to say I'm proud of you guys, man. I'm proud of you for your success. I mean not the NBA because that's just talent. But you have to find a way to figure out how am I going to make money the rest of my life. Keep doing your thing and thanks for having me.

KOBE BRYANT

KOBE: I can't believe you two guys are doing media.

MATT BARNES: Yeah, and doing it good too.

KOBE BRYANT: Doing great.

> And I'm very proud of you all. I want to give you all kudos for that because this is what we need. This is what we need in this world. —GARY PAYTON

GARY PAYTON

You're not talking like you're ignorant or a fool or nothing like that. You're talking where you all know about everything you're talking about in educational and doing things like that. And I'm very proud of you all. I want to give you all kudos for that because this is what we need. This is what we need in this world.

RIP HAMILTON

I'm happy to be here. Y'all killing it right now. Just to let y'all know that.

KENDRICK PERKINS

My wife was like, "Hold on, you're going on *All the Smoke*?" Hell yeah. She was like, "Shit, hell yeah, this is what I've been waiting on."

SHAQ

I want to congratulate y'all. I really love this show. This show speaks our language. It's actually the first show ever that speaks our language. I like the fact that you guys don't try to Bryant Gumbel it down. So congratulations and I hope you guys get many, many, many more awards.

KEVIN HART

KEVIN HART: I'm ready to talk. But before I get into that, flowers, man, season three, that's a big deal guys.

MATT BARNES: Thanks bro. Appreciate it.

KEVIN HART: Season three, man, you guys do an amazing job. That's why I'm here.

MATT BARNES: We appreciate that.

KEVIN HART: I'm here because of the platform, because of what the platform provides. You guys got a hell of an audience, and it's because of the job that you're doing. So I'll get that out the way.

MATT BARNES: Appreciate that.

LIL WAYNE

MATT BARNES: Hey, baby, we just want to tell you man, we feel like people don't get appreciated while they here, we want to appreciate them after they're gone. Man, you shaped the 2000s for us, man, for a lot of athletes, a lot of people growing up. You really inspired a lot of us, man. So we look up to you, man. We love you, we appreciate you. We want to let you know that, man, for sure.

LIL WAYNE: I appreciate that, man. With that said, though, man, with that said, coming up as well with myself coming up to you and Stack on the court. Just y'all, just that culture and keeping it alive and staying true to who y'all are on that court. That meant a lot just to a person that's not on that court and just watching it, man. Y'all shaped the nigga as well, man. Remember that man.

ALLEN IVERSON

ALLEN IVERSON: Y'all different, you know what I mean? And what makes y'all so excellent, and it's no disrespect to anybody that didn't play. It's no disrespect to them because there's dudes that know their shit, you know what I mean? That didn't play.

STEPHEN JACKSON: Yeah.

ALLEN IVERSON: But it's so different with y'all because y'all know all the feelings, the emotions, the locker room, you know what I mean? The media, y'all know it all. I'm so proud of you. You're talking about when we FaceTime and I'm crying and shit like that, but when I see you on Instagram and then when I see you on TV and doing your thing and standing up for us and all that, man, that's Steve. That's what he was bred to do, man. He is that. Man, just like you said all the time, you didn't ask to be put in this situation. It happened. And you took the responsibility and took off with it.

Hey, man, I appreciate y'all boys keep doing your thing being a voice for the real ones out here, man. Y'all do a great thing. —TRACY McGRADY

CHRIS BRICKLEY

I feel like when you guys started this podcast, people did be like, Oh, we'll see how it is. You guys have the best athletes in the world. You guys are doing it big. It's tough to be a player and then leave and then do something big post-career. It's tough and you guys are big-time.

SHAHEEN HOLLOWAY

Y'all platform. Real talk, the platform that you guys got, it's inspiring. Real talk, because you guys are yourself. Y'all not up here trying to be somebody different. And people see that and they feel that. And I think that's why y'all show us successful because dudes are looking at y'all like, Yo, that's me. I could do that. Look at all those dudes, they are real. So keep doing what y'all doing, bro. I've been trying to get on the show, man. I love what you guys are doing because y'all keeping it real, and y'all authentic. Don't change.

CHRIS BRICKLEY is one of the most sought-after and well-known trainers in all of basketball. A former walk-on at the University of Louisville who played under Rick Pitino, Brickley has trained NBA superstars such as LeBron James, Kevin Durant, and Kevin Love and women's collegiate greats Paige Bueckers and Azzi Fudd.

T.I.

T.I.: Man, respect both of you brothers. I appreciate the opportunity. It's an honor to sit here and just exchange dialogue with y'all. Both of y'all, I've seen both of y'all, go through some shit. And I was like, Oooh, I don't know how you going to get through that.

STEPHEN JACKSON: How you going to get out?

T.I.: Oooh, shit. Hey, man, the Goddamn palace brawl, bro. Like . . . Goddamn! This nigga got busy! You hear me? And you know what I'm saying, man? You had to exercise so much restraint then.

STEVEN JACKSON: A couple times.

T.I.: So I respect, I've seen y'all be tested, you know what I'm saying? Not necessarily by the world as much as tested by yourselves. When you had to overcome yourself, you had to really be who you presented yourself to be, you know what I'm saying? And y'all pass it. That's what real motherfuckers are going to respect.

When you think of Seton Hall, you think of SHAHEEN HOLLOWAY, who was a star player for the Pirates and the current head coach of the program. The MVP of the 1996 McDonald's All-American Boys Game, Holloway had an international career in which he played in seven different countries before joining the coaching ranks as an assistant at Iona. He coached the Saint Peter's men's team that made the Elite Eight in the 2021–22 season, before taking the job at his alma mater.

STAK 5
NBA CHAMPION 14 SEASONS

MATT BARNES
NBA CHAMPION 14 SEASONS

I want to congratulate y'all. I really love this show.

—SHAQ

It's an honor to sit here and just exchange dialogue with y'all. —T.I.

MAGIC JOHNSON

When brothers are doing great things, that empowers me too. Right? Right. So, remember that. So listen, this show is unbelievable and they talk about they wasn't superstars, no, they're superstars. See, you don't have to always be the best at one thing. See, that's not the mark of a great man, it's whether you could be the best at other things or two things or three things. How can you reinvent yourself? Man, you guys are killing it, killing it, killing it, killing it.

RICKY WILLIAMS

I appreciate what you guys are doing because we need it.

DOC RIVERS

I'm so happy with what you guys are doing. Without our voices this stuff would get swept under the rug.

TAYLOR ROOKS

Yes, before we end, I do want to say shout-out to you guys because you guys have done something that is really hard to do in media, which is create an environment. People come on here, they know they can be themselves, they can talk freely, they're with their peers. If they have anything they want to get off their chest in a way that will work, they come here. So just shout-out to y'all for making a transition that people underestimate how difficult it is to make. I love this show. I love what you guys mean to sports and to culture. So thank you for having me.

I love this show. I love what you guys mean to sports and to culture. So thank you for having me. —TAYLOR ROOKS

MICHAEL RAPAPORT

I love you guys and I love the show. And I'm so not surprised that you guys are banging and doing your shit.

CHARLAMAGNE THA GOD

CHARLAMAGNE THA GOD: **ALL THE SMOKE** needs its network where they're just rolling out those voices in sports that are like you all. Only you all know that. Only Matt and Stephen know who those other voices are that are like you all, those guys that are cut from that cloth.

STEPHEN JACKSON: They're attracted to us, yeah.

CHARLAMAGNE THA GOD: Absolutely. That's why this show works. Plenty of sports guys have gotten together and done the shows. We've never seen sports from a real nigga perspective. That's just the truth of it.

LENARD LARRY McKELVEY, better known as **CHARLAMAGNE THA GOD**, has been hosting the syndicated radio show *The Breakfast Club* in New York City since 2010. He founded the Black Effect Podcast Network, hosted his own late-night talk show, and was inducted into the Radio Hall of Fame in 2020.

Words from the
ALL THE SMOKE Crew

ISAAC OLEXIO: I remember the day Matt and Stak first showed up to shoot the **ALL THE SMOKE** promo. Within the first hour the room was filled with thick smoke and side-splitting laughter. None of us had any idea how many legendary interviews and lifelong memories would be created in that room. Through rapid growth we've been able to retain the raw essence of the show. I'm immensely proud to be a part of this team, and we're just getting started!

BRIAN DAILEY: We knew we were creating a show that would resonate with fans and give them something they hadn't seen before. But **ATS** quickly grew into something way beyond. It's a brand rooted in real conversations and authentic storytelling. **ATS** has changed the definition of authentic content by giving heroes a place to be humanized and rewrite the narratives placed on them by others. The world quickly flocked to see their favorite stars in a new light; as their authentic selves.

RICH CRISOL: Controlling the narrative has been the mission since 2019. It's been an honor and privilege to share the same room with Matt and Stak. From the talent to the crew behind the scenes, the energy and creativity continues to level up each season and create content that resonates for all.

JIM PORTELA: Working on **ALL THE SMOKE** has been the most rewarding experience of my career so far. From top to bottom the team is the best in the business. Matt and Stak are as candid with us off camera as they are with the guests on camera, and that's something I really respect. It's been my privilege to be here since day one.

JELANI McCOY: The best part about this shit is coming to set doing something that's never been done before, then realizing we're not even who we're supposed to be yet.

NICK SHAVATT, a.k.a. RAZOR BLADE CHAMP: Matt, Stack, BD, and E imagined and created maybe the best sports talk show ever! Inclusion in a movement like this is why I do what I do! What else is there to say, except thank you!

DYLAN DREYFUSS: Being able to play a part in **ALL THE SMOKE** has been the experience of a lifetime. I'll cherish these memories forever. Love and respect to Matt, Stak, and everyone who plays a role in making the show possible.

GENE O. DAVIS: **ALL THE SMOKE** has been amazing to witness from its inception. Watching it thrive in this competitive space has been more than refreshing. Matt and Stak are the bar of what a successful podcast and brand should strive to be like. My favorite memory is undoubtedly the Earvin "Magic" Johnson live show they did at the Beverly Hilton. Imagine watching your childhood hero being interviewed by your best friends. Nothing but respect and love for the people who work tirelessly to make this show as successful as it has become, and I'm proud to be a part of it.

NATHAN BRONSON: Been a true blessing to have the opportunity to work with Matt and Stak and the whole **ATS** family. **ALL THE SMOKE** have really cemented themselves in the podcast space and after 200+ episodes, I know this is just the beginning.

DAN LOVI: **ALL THE SMOKE** stands out from the crowd for a countless number of reasons. The one that reverberates the most with me is the coming together of people from all walks of life. From the late-night hustle to the celebratory moments, we always have been and always will be all in it together.

ERIC NEWMAN: **ALL THE SMOKE** from day one always felt like more than just a show. We knew it was something the masses were looking for as Matt and Stak are both so

unique in terms of their journeys and how they connect with both the guests and the audience. The opportunity to play a role in building **ATS** has been an incredible privilege and responsibility. The community and culture that's been built around the show is incomparable to anything else out there.

RAY YOUNG: **ATS** is a family show. That's been the secret sauce. Meaning everybody involved acts as family members who all want the best for the show. That energy touches our guests, which allows them to relax and feel at ease before the conversation on camera ever happens.

CHRISTINA NOTARMUZI: I started working with the **ALL THE SMOKE** team in 2021 when everything was still "virtual." Even then, from behind my laptop, this team felt like a family. As the show grew, the team grew and we worked together to be the best in the game. I'm so proud of everything we've done and it's been an honor to work beside such talented athletes, hosts, producers, and creatives. I can't wait to take on this next chapter.

Acknowledgments

THANK YOU TO OUR FANS. WITHOUT YOU,
THIS WOULDN'T BE POSSIBLE.

Episode Index

About the Authors

MATT BARNES scrapped and clawed his way through fourteen NBA seasons, which included a championship in 2017 with the Golden State Warriors. He is a father of six (soon to be seven), the co-host of the series **ALL THE SMOKE**, the CEO of All the Smoke Productions, and an investor/advisor for several companies.

STEPHEN JACKSON played fourteen NBA seasons and was known for his infectious confidence and charisma. His career included a championship in 2003 with the San Antonio Spurs. He is the co-host of the series **ALL THE SMOKE** and has emerged as a spokesman for human rights and equality for people all around the world.